▌▐ ▌▐▐▌▐ ▌▐▐▌▐▐▌▐▐▌ ▐ ▌▐

↻ **W9-AZE-297**

QUOTATIONS
F R O M
SPEAKER
N E W T

THE LITTLE RED, WHITE AND BLUE BOOK OF THE REPUBLICAN REVOLUTION

Amy D. Bernstein and Peter W. Bernstein, Editors
Research by Gary Cohen

WORKMAN PUBLISHING, NEW YORK

Copyright © 1995 by Peter W. Bernstein Corporation

All rights reserved. No portion of this book may be reproduced—
mechanically, electronically, or by any other means including
photocopying—without written permission of the publisher.
Published simultaneously in Canada by Thomas Allen & Son, Ltd.

Material from "Renewing American Civilization" provided by
permission from The Progress & Freedom Foundation,
1250 H St. NW, Washington DC 20005. For further information
about Renewing American Civilization, call 1-800-TO-RENEW.

Workman books are available at special discount when purchased
in bulk for special sales promotions as well as fundraising or
educational use. Special book excerpts or editions can also be
created to specification. For details, contact the Special Sales
Director at the address below.

Workman Publishing Company, Inc.
708 Broadway
New York, NY 10003

First printing January 1995

Manufactured in the United States
10 9 8 7 6 5 4 3 2 1

To Alex and Ele and all
the other Republicans
in the family.

ACKNOWLEDGMENTS

Bob Bernstein, publisher, father, father-in-law and grandfather extraordinaire, was the creative spark for this book.

Gary Cohen was indefatigable in tracking down every detail, Mike Barone generously and expeditiously penned an introduction. The following also helped track down material and made useful suggestions: Doug Cumming of *The Atlanta Constitution*; Joe and Emily Cumming in Carrollton, Georgia; Myron House and the staff of the Ingram Library at West Georgia College; Tim Russert of NBC's *Meet the Press*; Frank Gregorsky; David Worley; Jeffrey Eisenach and the Progress & Freedom Foundation for providing videotapes and transcripts of Renewing American Civilization; Barbara Hohvach of the Heritage Foundation; Lisa Nelson of GOPAC; Dan Buck; the Research Department of the Democratic National Committee; Sarah Halsted; Luke Mitchell; Ron Wilson; Anna Mulrine and Cecily Slocum.

Merrill McLoughlin, Mike Ruby, Chris Ma, Cornelia Carter and Jill Shadick—all colleagues at

U.S. News & World Report—provided warm encouragement and kindly support. Peter Olberg gave us expert counsel. Peter Workman, Sally Kovalchick, Lynn Strong and Ruth Hochbaum made everything happen.

Our thanks to all.

INTRODUCTION

Newt Gingrich struck like a thunderclap on the national scene when Republicans won control of the House of Representatives in November 1994, making him the first Republican Speaker of the House in 40 years. But Gingrich has been making rumbling noises in national politics, with varying reverberations, for two decades now. And he has shown both a consistency and an originality unusual in an electoral politician. Nevertheless, Gingrich remains an unknown to most Americans at a time when he is second in the line of succession to the presidency and one of the most powerful politicians in the United States.

Who is Newt Gingrich? What does he believe in? And what impact will he have on American politics?

First and perhaps foremost, Gingrich is an American exceptionalist, a believer in the idea widely shared by American voters but widely doubted by American intellectual elites that this is a uniquely good nation with a special mission in world history. Other contemporary American leaders—among them Bill Clinton, just three years Gingrich's junior—found their faith in America's goodness undermined by the civil rights struggle and the Vietnam war. Not Gingrich. The stepson of an army sergeant, he grew up on military bases, the most American of environments overseas as well as at home. He was largely insulated from the civil rights struggle—the military was and is the most integrated part of American society. When the Vietnam war was raging, Gingrich, as the married father of two children, was eligible for a deferment from the draft. Unlike Clinton, he never had to worry about facing a draft board. His certitude in the moral rightness of America's role in the world remained unblemished.

The second thing to note about Gingrich is that he is the promoter of an energetic government, propagating what he considers mainstream American values: hard work, perseverance, equality of opportunity, entrepreneurial free enterprise. As a history professor at a small state college and a member of Congress, he is a creature of the public sector of the economy, yet that's not where he sees America's strength. He argues forcefully for promoting high technology as well as restoring traditional values. An active government can do both, he says, spending more on defense against the enemies of American values, more on space exploration that will boost American spirits as well as high-tech know-how, and less on a welfare system that demoralizes its recipients and fosters a criminal underclass. Unashamedly, he says government should require patriotic ceremonies like pledging allegiance to the flag. School prayer should be sought, not shunned. Yet for Gingrich, the nation is more than the government. He seeks to replace the Democrats' "Liberal Welfare State" with what he calls "a Conservative Opportunity Society."

Finally, Gingrich has always been a fighter, not a compromiser, always ready for a brawl against his political adversaries on both sides of the aisle. If Bill Clinton has tried to mollify and appease, Newt Gingrich has never shied from confrontation. He ran for Congress three times before he finally won in 1978. At a time when Democrats held almost two-thirds of the seats and the presidency as well, Gingrich declared that his goal was to win a Republican majority in the House. In pursuit of that dream, he took on two powerful Speakers: Tip O'Neill was embarrassed and Jim Wright was forced to resign.

Gingrich likes to provoke, to say or do something that will make his ideological adversaries bristle and, he hopes, the voter take notice. Former House Republican leader Bob Michel once told him that he shouldn't feel that he had to have an opinion on every subject. The paternal advice has been ignored. Gingrich speaks with a fluency and self-assuredness that makes him a tough debater, sprinkling his opinions with a formidable command of historical fact and analogy. His style of discourse, with his four- and five-point lists and catchy phrases, resembles the patter of business management best-sellers or promotional motivators. And he's clever, deliberate and disciplined. For years, in certain Democratic liberal circles it has been popular to dismiss Gingrich as the latest right-wing nut. That's a mistake.

Gingrich, I wrote in 1987, is "something of an American Gaullist." Like Charles de Gaulle, he has believed from childhood that he has a great destiny, that he will reshape the nation. Like De Gaulle, he has overcome setbacks, mistakes, ridicule and opposition, and has persevered in his stands until his confidence no longer seems ridiculous. Like De Gaulle, he believes that his nation has a special mission. And like De Gaulle, he has heaped scorn on his opponents and cold-bloodedly ended the careers of those who have stood in his way. Gingrich cannot be unaware of the parallels—in one of his lectures he talks about De Gaulle and himself in the same breath.

The analogy at some point breaks down: the United States is not France; 1994 is not 1940; the post that Gingrich has won in our system is not equal to the posts De Gaulle assumed; Gingrich is a populist, De Gaulle an elitist. Gingrich's strengths have sometimes been his weaknesses. His nationalism has led him to unfairly question his opponents' good faith; his vision of what government should do has been undercut on occasion by his own tactical maneuverings; his attacks on others' ethics have stimulated attacks on his own, some not entirely without basis. Many of his own proposals are as fraught with weaknesses as those of his adversaries whom he so viciously attacks. The history teacher who keeps his students awake with some provocative remarks could become the political leader who brings himself down with others.

But a professor-turned-politician can also be an effective leader, as Woodrow Wilson and Daniel Patrick Moynihan have shown. He can frame issues by setting out a vision or by leading attacks, as Gingrich has done over the years. He can set out an agenda for action, as Gingrich did in the Contract with America in September 1994. There can be little doubt that there would be no Republican majority in the House in 1995 but for the vision, strategy and tactics of Newt Gingrich in 1994 and for many years before.

Now that he has reached his lifetime goal and is Speaker, Gingrich must not only teach; he must act, and keep promises, and get results. Those acts can be understood better by reflecting on his words, before and just after he came to national attention in the thunderclap of November 1994.

Michael Barone
Senior writer, *U.S. News & World Report*
Co-author, *The Almanac of American Politics*

CONTENTS

THE LIFE AND TIMES OF NEWTON LEROY GINGRICH

1943 — Born June 17 to Newton Leroy Robert McPherson and Kathleen Daugherty McPherson in Harrisburg, Pa. According to his mother's account, the marriage lasted three days: "We were married on a Saturday and I left him on a Tuesday. I got Newtie in those three days."

1946 — Kathleen marries army Lt. Col. Robert Bruce Gingrich, who adopts Newt. ("Newtie is a talker; Bob is not," Kathleen said recently, recalling the relationship between her son and his stepfather.) Newt attends army base schools in Kansas and, during his father's tours of duty abroad, in Orléans, France, and Stuttgart, West Germany.

1961 — Graduates from Newton D. Baker High School in Columbus, Ga. During high school, he developed a crush on his 23-year-old math teacher, Jacqueline Battley, seven years his senior. Gingrich enrolls at Emory University in

Atlanta, where Jackie has taken a teaching position. He shows up at her door and asks for a date.

1962—On June 19, at age 19, Newt marries Jackie. In the next four years, he and Jackie have two daughters, Linda Kathleen and Jacqueline Sue.

1965—Gingrich graduates from Emory and goes on to receive a master's degree from Tulane University in 1968 and a Ph.D. in modern European history in 1971. (His Ph.D. dissertation topic: Belgium's Education Policy in the Congo, 1945–60.) At Tulane, he accepts student draft deferments during the Vietnam war, tries marijuana and is one of the student leaders of a demonstration defending the school paper's right to print a photograph of a nude male faculty member. In 1968 he joins New York Governor Nelson Rockefeller's presidential campaign because of the governor's support of civil rights.

1970—While completing his doctorate, Gingrich joins the faculty of West Georgia College of

Carrollton, Ga. After a year, he unsuccessfully attempts to become chairman of his department.

1974—Gingrich challenges Democratic Congressman John J. Flynt, Jr., of Georgia's 6th Congressional District and loses by some 2,800 votes. Encouraged, he tries again in 1976, losing by an even narrower margin. During the '76 campaign, he attacks Flynt, a member of the House Ethics Committee, for not being tough enough in enforcing ethics violations by Congressmen—the first of many Gingrich attacks on Democrats for their lax ethics.

1978—At age 35, Gingrich wins election to the House of Representatives after Flynt retires. He runs on a platform of lower taxes and opposition to the Panama Canal Treaty.

1982—He and Jackie divorce. Shortly afterward, he marries Marianne Ginther.

1983—The Conservative Opportunity Society, a group of House Republicans and the vehicle that first brings Gingrich to national prominence, takes shape.

1984—Gingrich publishes *Window of Opportunity: A Blueprint for the Future*, written with Marianne Gingrich and science fiction writer David Drake. The book, which lays out Gingrich's philosophy, argues, among other things, that space exploration can solve the world's most pressing problems. At the time of publication, Gingrich is chairman of the Congressional Space Caucus.

In May, Gingrich is at the center of a partisan battle with Speaker Thomas (Tip) O'Neill. Gingrich reads a report on the floor of the House criticizing Democratic foreign policy statements, pausing periodically as if to give his targets a chance to respond. With the C-Span TV camera focused on Gingrich, it appears that the Democrats have nothing to say in their defense. Later, a furious O'Neill orders the TV cameras to pan the empty chamber during "special orders" and lambasts Gingrich's tactics—"the lowest thing that I have ever seen in my 32 years in Congress." O'Neill's use of the word "lowest" is ruled out of order and stricken from the House record for lack of comity. The incident makes the TV networks' evening news.

1986—Gingrich takes over GOPAC, a political action committee that supports Republican candidates in state and local races.

1987—Gingrich attacks the ethics of House Speaker Jim Wright of Texas, calling for an investigation into some of his financial dealings. One charge: a book contract signed by Wright circumvented House limitations on outside income. In April 1989, the House Ethics Committee releases a report accusing Wright of violating House rules in at least 69 instances. On May 31, 1989, Wright announces his resignation from the House.

1989—Gingrich is elected Republican House Whip, the No. 2 leadership position, by a two-vote margin.

In April, a month after his election, Gingrich is the subject of a House Ethics Committee probe. The 10-count complaint charged that Gingrich violated House rules on outside gifts and income by benefiting from two partnerships that helped finance two books—an unfinished novel and *Window of Opportunity*. In July, Gingrich becomes the subject of a second ethics probe alleging that he took two staff members off his Congressional payroll to work on his reelection campaigns in 1986 and 1988, and then returned them to the payroll after the election with significant, though temporary, increases in salary. House rules bar granting temporary year-end raises that can be construed as bonuses. Eventually, the Ethics Committee decides not to pursue either investigation.

1990—Gingrich opposes the 1990 budget deal in which President George Bush agrees to tax increases. In October, the budget deal is defeated by the House.

Gingrich faces a tough reelection challenge from Democrat David Worley, winning by only 974 votes.

1991—In the wake of a scandal over the House Bank, it is revealed that Gingrich had overdrafts for 22 checks—one for $9,463 sent to the IRS. Later in the year, Gingrich opts to give up his chauffeur-driven Lincoln town car, a traditional perk for House Whips.

1992—Redistricting by the Democrat-controlled Georgia Legislature dramatically alters the shape of Gingrich's Congressional District in suburban Atlanta. The new district is overwhelmingly white (93% vs. 80% in the old 6th District) and heavily Republican. In the fall election, Gingrich wins comfortably, defeating Tony Center.

1994—Republicans gain control of the House and Senate in the November 8 election, aided by the 10-point Contract with America, reflecting Gingrich philosophies and setting the stage for Gingrich to become Speaker of the House in January.

1995—Gingrich is formally elected Speaker of the House, the first Republican to hold the post in more than 40 years.

PART I
THE CALL TO REVOLUTION

Newt Gingrich's beginnings were not auspicious. Conceived in a three-day marriage between a 17-year-old mother and a 19-year-old father, he lived for his first three years with his single mother and grandparents. His mother's second husband, a career military man who adopted Newt, was a stern authority figure. While living with his family in France, he visited the World War I battlefield at Verdun and experienced an epiphany; he decided at that moment he would try to change the world by becoming a politician instead of a paleontologist. During high school in Stuttgart, West Germany, he wrote a 180-page paper on the balance of global power. He began telling friends that he would one day run for

Congress and save Western civilization. By his own account, he was "pretty weird as a kid."

Gingrich's experiences as an impressionable army brat in cold-war Europe profoundly affected his view of the world as an unsafe place. It also has developed in him a near-Manichaean vision of politics as a fight between all good and all evil that has suffused his dramatic political rhetoric throughout his career. He is a crusader whose battles at times are, like Don Quixote's, mostly in his mind. He approaches every contest as if it were a war and does not flinch from inflicting pain on his opponent. To Gingrich, who has been seen stalking the halls of the legislature with a copy of a book on war strategy under his arm, all seems fair in love and war; the tactical advantage is the key to winning, and winning is the absolute goal.

Not that success came easily. Gingrich has succeeded by carefully mapping out and fulfilling his objectives, and by doing his homework. Like his own father, he married at 19. By the end of graduate school, he, his wife and two children were a fully formed political team: Jackie Gingrich and their daughters were integral to Candidate Gingrich's image as a God-fearing, family-values man, a deacon and Sunday School teacher at the local Baptist church. Hardworking and of very modest means (even today his latest financial disclosure forms reveal total assets for him and his spouse of between $19,000 and $110,000), Gingrich and his family seemed at the time to be model members of the Carrollton, Georgia, community, where he was an associate professor at West Georgia College and whence he began his quest for elective office. It took three campaigns before Gingrich was able to win a seat in Congress. Winning proved a fortunate outcome. His preoccupation with politics had foreclosed any chance that he would be granted tenure.

All the while, Gingrich was formulating his political philosophy, arriving at a blend of ideas that were refined over years of academic and political debate. He was never interested in the conventional wisdom. According to a former professor, Gingrich was "always attracted to the revisionist theory of history, whatever deviated from the norm." While still in graduate school he taught a non-credit course on the year 2000, and at West Georgia College he developed an environmental studies program and a course in futurism. His house in Carrollton was a favorite gathering place, where students would go for pig roasts and, as one student recalled, to "drink wine, talk about the future, the environment, big-picture stuff." The distillation of those and countless other sessions and years of eclectic readings is a seemingly potent mixture. His point of departure is a call to shake the American system to its very roots by reforming American culture, American politics and the American soul.

1. GROWING UP

I'm not sitting here as someone who is unfamiliar with the late 20th century. . . . I know life can be complicated.

The New York Times
November 24, 1994

I spent probably into my forties coping with the whole process of being adopted and having to sort it out. Marianne helped me come to grips with being human at that level, because I had literally dealt with all sorts of issues by making them mechanical and outside myself.

The Washington Post
June 12, 1989

Having been an army brat, I know how exciting military life can be.

"News from Congressman Newt Gingrich"
October 2, 1982

There is probably a part of me that has been lonely . . . for large parts of my life. You'd move every 18 months and so would your best friend, so you would have that churning. But I do have a network of personal friends that is very deep and very real.

Commenting on life as an army brat.
The Washington Post
June 12, 1989

I read part of the book [*The Great Santini,* a Pat Conroy novel about a son's attempts to please his military father] and couldn't finish it. It was too frightening.

The Washington Post
June 12, 1989

I was born a Lutheran, raised in a general Protestant environment in the U.S. military where you basically were whatever the chaplain was. I was, I think, a Methodist acolyte at one point, and I converted and became a Baptist.

Renewing American Civilization, Class 1

I'm the guy in the eighth grade who did not go across the floor and ask the girl to dance for two reasons. One is, she might say no and I'd be embarrassed; two, she might say yes and I'd have to dance.

The Washington Post
January 3, 1985

I got active in this business of politics and self-government in 1958, when my father, who was serving in the U.S. Army, took us to the battlefield of Verdun.

Vanity Fair
July 1989

It [visiting Verdun] literally changed my life. I came to the conclusion . . . that threats to civilization are real, that the quality of leadership is a major factor in whether civilization survives. So I sort of changed my goal from zoo director or vertebrate paleontologist to being a leader.

The Philadelphia Inquirer
November 6, 1994

My father was a soldier then, and the house we lived in was right across from the Seventh Army Headquarters. Late at night he would get a call, and in the early morning hours the entire headquarters would move into the field. I could see it all from my bedroom window—tanks, trucks, armed personnel carriers. It gradually dawned on me that this wasn't a game. In a sense, my mother, my sisters, and I were being held hostage to world power. Faced with this, I began to wonder what it was all about, why my father was risking his life, why my country was in danger.

Recalling life at age 14 on the army base in Stuttgart, West Germany.
Campaign profile
(Ingram Library, West Georgia College)
1976

I think I was very lonely and I think I was very driven. . . . If you decide in your freshman year in high school that your job is to spend your lifetime trying to change the future of your people, you're probably fairly weird. I think I was pretty weird as a kid.

The Washington Post
January 3, 1985

Jackie [Blattley] was my math teacher in high school and it really made a tremendous amount of sense to marry at the time, when I was a freshman in college. Who you are at 19 may not be who you are at 39. We were married not quite a year when Kathy was born, so I had a daughter in my sophomore year with all the economic pressures that implies, and then Jackie Sue was born when I was in graduate school.

The Washington Post
January 3, 1985

My stepfather taught me all the wrong reasons [for marriage]. Exactly the right lessons for being a good combat officer in the infantry—which may not be as helpful for living with your wife as you might think.

The Washington Post
June 12, 1989

If you live your life as a hostage to every-body else's decision, you either have to live a very narrow life or you have to spend a lot of time in pain. I hoped my mother would come, but I also understood that she . . . had to live with my stepfather. She only had to love me. . . . I never held it against her. I never held it against him.

Commenting on his parents' refusal to attend his wedding to Jackie Battley, who was seven years his senior.
The Washington Post
December 18, 1994

I went to Columbus College and Emory University and on to graduate school at Georgia State University and then to Tulane University, where both a National Defense Education Act Fellowship and a scholarship from the state of Georgia helped me complete my Ph.D.

Speech, "Creating a Learning Society for America's 21st Century" (Papers of David Worley) November 14, 1986

10

Given everything I believe in, a large part of me thinks I should have gone over [to Vietnam]. . . . Part of the question I had to ask myself was what difference I would have made. No one felt that this was the battle-line on which freedom would live or die. Tragically, it was the kind of war fought in the U.S. Congress, not the battlefield.

**Commenting on his decision
to take a draft deferment.**
The Wall Street Journal
February 11, 1985

The historical record is that 19 years ago, I used marijuana once at a party . . . in New Orleans. . . . It didn't have any effect on me. As a matter of fact, I never went back and revisited it.

The Washington Post
November 8, 1987

[My ambition] is to be an old-time political boss in 20 years.

**Recalling his days as an organizer of the Young
Republicans at Emory University in the '60s.**
The Atlanta Journal
July 22, 1974

2. THE RISE TO POWER

I made the decision very early that I was never going to get tenure [at West Georgia College in Carrollton, Georgia], that I was going to be a politician. I was tempted to apply for tenure after I lost [for Congress] twice. I went to see the dean, who was a good friend, who always supported me politically, and he said, "Run for office—you're not going to get tenure under any circumstances. You've spent four years campaigning; you can't turn now and say 'Let me get back on track.'"

The Washington Post
June 12, 1985

My wife, Jackie, and I have spent a number of years working with young people both through my profession as a teacher and once again as we both teach at our Church's Sunday School. These years have taught us the importance of setting an example in all the things that we might do or attempt to do, an example that would help our young people believe in the Georgia virtues of honesty, sincerity and integrity. I don't think it is asking too much when the American people want their public officials to practice those virtues and to live a Christian life.

Gingrich "Congressgram," issued during his
second unsuccessful election campaign
(Ingram Library, West Georgia College)
Spring 1976

"If you like welfare cheaters, you'll love Virginia Shapard."

Campaign flyer (Ingram Library, West Georgia
College), 1978. The flyer went on to
point out that Democratic opponents
Virginia Shapard and Atlanta black leader
Julian Bond opposed a welfare reform bill.

"When elected, Newt will keep his family together."

1978 campaign ad. Opponent Virginia Shapard had indicated that she would move to Washington while her family remained in Georgia.
Mother Jones
November 1984

One of the reasons I ended up getting a divorce [from Jackie] was that if I was disintegrating enough as a person that I could not say [things in public that were consistent with my private life], then I needed to get my life straight, not quit saying them. And I think that literally was the crisis I came to. I guess I look back on it a little bit like somebody who's in Alcoholics Anonymous—it was a very, very bad period of my life, and it had been getting steadily worse. . . . I ultimately wound up at a point where probably suicide or going insane or divorce were the last three options.

Mother Jones
November 1984

All I can say is when you've been talking about divorce for 11 years and you've gone to a marriage counselor, and the other person doesn't want the divorce, I'm not sure there is any sensitive way to handle it.

The Washington Post
January 3, 1985

I'm willing to say, having gone through the last five and six years and having understood that—as an incorrigible bulldozer—it's conceivable I was that insensitive. It was never in any sense deliberate.

Commenting on the story that he asked for a divorce while Jackie was in the hospital recovering from a cancer operation.
The Washington Post
June 12, 1989

I understood totally that in my hometown and among people who knew me, there would be a lot of people who would be very cynical [about the divorce and his remarriage several months later to Marianne Ginther] and would say, "Who does he think he is?" And part of my conclusion is the same one I'm sure you run into. If the only people allowed to write news stories were those who had never told a lie, we wouldn't have many stories. If the only people allowed to serve on juries were saints, we wouldn't have any juries. And I thought there was a clear distinction between my private life and the deliberate use of a position of authority to seduce and abuse somebody in your care. And I would draw that distinction.

I would say to you unequivocally—it will probably sound pious and sanctimonious saying it—I am a sinner. I am a normal person. I am like everyone else I ever met. One of the reasons I go to God is that I ain't very good—I'm not perfect.

Mother Jones
November 1984

16

Think of me as a backbencher who used to work very hard trying to figure out how can I articulate something in a flashy enough way so the press can pick it up. Now all of a sudden I have this microphone, and when I yell it comes across like a painful noise because the system is now geared to carry me.

That's requiring that I change my style. I will be somewhat less confrontational, and somewhat less abrasive in the future because I am no longer the person I once was. A Newt Gingrich press conference or interview is now potentially a real news story. That means I can be much quieter, much more positive. And so I'll change. And it will take two to five years for my reputation to catch up and in some ways it never will. There are scars I have made in the last two or three years that will be with me through the rest of my career.

**Commenting on his sudden rise to prominence
among House Republicans.**
The Washington Post
January 3, 1985

It's not altruism! It's not altruism! I have an enormous personal ambition. I want to shift the entire planet. And I'm doing it. Ronald Reagan uses the term "opportunity society" and that didn't exist four years ago. . . . I'm unavoidable . . . I represent real power.

The Washington Post
January 3, 1985

If I had any single regret, because of my total misunderstanding, I helped cause Marianne her back problem that was almost crippling in 1986 and 1987. By not being there, by not understanding. She was going to school very intently and graduating *magna cum laude* and I was misunderstanding the stress she was under and adding my own stress to it.

When you have a game which is this passionate and this intense and this exhausting, it's just very hard to have a personal relationship. It probably attracts people who in part get their ego needs from a larger audience—because they're too frightened to get it from a smaller audience.

The Washington Post
June 12, 1989

Marianne has no interest in being married to The Whip. She'd like to be married to Newt. And sometimes we have a very difficult time transitioning back and forth.

Atlanta Magazine
January 1990

You talk about crying! The spring of 1988, I spent a fair length of time trying to come to grips with who I was and the habits I had, and what they did to people that I truly loved. I really spent a period of time where, I suspect, I cried three or four times a week. I read *Men Who Hate Women and the Women Who Love Them* and I found frightening pieces that related to . . . my own life.

In the same newspaper article, Marianne revealed that their marriage had been "off and on" for some time. Gingrich himself said that the marriage had a 53-47 chance of lasting.
The Washington Post
June 12, 1989

I mean, I train to be dominant in a fight with Jim Wright [Speaker of the House of Representatives whom Gingrich attacked as being corrupt] and then I walk into a room with a normal human being [Marianne] who's brilliant and wonderful and that stuff, but she doesn't gear up every morning to be a viking! I mean, that's not her world. When she's pleasant, she points out that I'm incorrigible, which simply means that you knock me on the mat and I get up again, you knock me on the mat and I get up again. And after a while, if you're a normal human being, you get tired of knocking me down and so you give in, but then *you're* really angry because you just knocked me down nine times and I *still* won. And they can be things as simple as "What do you want for dinner?" or "What do you want to do this weekend?"

The Washington Post
June 12, 1989

There were days when I was doing something like filing [ethics] charges against the Speaker of the House [Jim Wright] and I was the only person doing it. And when my wife and I walked down the corridor to sign the papers—which I thought was great courage on her part, because it wasn't her fight—you had that real sense of being, this is really history, and I'm really alone.

Renewing American Civilization, Class 6

I am not a pathologically confrontational person. And I am not in any significant way an extremist. I was a backbencher who knew that in order to be effective, you had to use certain techniques.

Atlanta Magazine
January 1990

One of the things that people never understood about my rise [to House Republican Whip in the 103rd Congress] is that I carried moderate *and* conservative activists. But, in fact, I carried the moderates. So I am a right-wing, southern Republican hard-line politician—who swept *New England* in the Whip race. . . . It was a totally implausible coalition *unless* you understood that the underlying secret was activism—not being hard-line ideologically but being aggressive and having positive ideas.

The Washington Blade
November 25, 1994

I'm the whip; that has lots of advantages. I have a reputation, so when I give a speech or make a tape, people are likely to listen to me. . . . it's getting easier for me. It's not quite as brutal.

The Washington Post
June 12, 1989

If you said to me, "What are your hobbies?," they would be reading, going to the movies, going for long walks, animals and the outdoors. But the truth is when I read, I am reading about

something that relates. When I go to the movies
—I saw *Parenthood* the other day—I think,
"What does that tell me about America?" In a
sense, I am almost always engaged. And that has
a disadvantage to really break out of that and
stop and think, "All right, how do you have a
private life?"

You see, I really *like* this game.

Atlanta Magazine
January 1990

I had to go home and sit down and look at a
970-vote margin and ask myself, "If I am convinced I represent the values of my district—and
I am—what was I failing to communicate?"

And then I took all of the fancy things which
in the abstract are exactly right in Washington
and I realized that if you were in Jonesboro,
Georgia, none of them made any sense at all.
They were all college professor stuff. . . . if you
were a normal voter back home you'd say,
"Yeah, but what does it mean to me today?"

Commenting on his narrow victory in 1990.
The Washington Times
March 6, 1991

I'll do almost anything to win a Republican majority in the Congress.

Los Angeles Times
August 25, 1991

This [the 1992 Congressional campaign] is the most miserable campaign I've ever been in. I've seriously considered just quitting, just saying, "This filth is so sickening, I don't want to be part of it anymore."

**Response to charges by Democratic opponent
Tony Center, who ran ads about the details of
the breakup of Gingrich's first marriage.**
The New York Times
October 29, 1992

The price of trying to have historic change is to take historic risks. We had a good friend tell us the other week—somebody who knows the Clinton White House very intimately—"You should be mildly paranoid" because I really am Public Enemy Number One in the building. They just go nuts. But you can't be mildly paranoid and be effective.

The Washington Post
October 25, 1994

24

I think I am a transformational figure. I think I am trying to effect a change so large that the people who would be hurt by the change, the liberal machine, have a natural reaction. . . . I think because I'm so systematically purposeful about changing our world. . . . I'm a much tougher partisan than they've [the Democrats] seen . . . much more intense, much more persistent, much more willing to take risks to get it done.

Comment in an October 17 interview
on his role as a "lightning rod."
The Washington Post
December 20, 1994

The first thing I did [the morning of being voted in as Republican leader and consequently the next Speaker of the House], frankly, after getting up was I called my mom and dad. My stepfather served this country for 27 years as an infantryman and in that sense has some identity with Bob Michel [retiring Minority Leader of the House]. And I thanked both of them for all the things they have done over the years. . . . I particularly wanted to chat with my dad because I think that at levels that we had never talked much about—it's one of the characteristics of infantrymen that they don't exactly emote lots of things—and I talked about the fact that I think his intensity and his commitment and his deep belief in what he had done to preserve freedom were in fact integral to what I had learned from him and why I would be here today.

Speech at the Capitol,
Washington, D.C.
December 5, 1994

As a historian I understand how histories are written. My enemies will write histories that dismiss me and prove I was unimportant. My friends will write histories that glorify me and prove I was more important than I was. And two generations or three from now, some serious, sober historian will write a history that sort of implies I was whoever I was.

The Washington Post
January 3, 1985

3. THE REPUBLICAN REVOLUTION: OVERTHROWING THE WELFARE STATE

I'm not interested in preserving the status quo; I want to overthrow it.

Los Angeles Times Magazine
August 25, 1991

Let me say that I come to you as a revolutionary, and I mean that word very deliberately and very explicitly. . . . it is impossible for us to truly have the kind of country we want without going through a peaceful political revolution. . . . I use the word deliberately in the sense that Jefferson meant when he said that every generation needs its own revolution.

I used the word deliberately in the sense that Lincoln in his first inaugural meant when he said the American people have every right politically to have a revolution. Our revolution ought to be at the ballot box. . . .

I believe that revolution is necessary. I can't imagine America being successful and safe and prosperous in the 21st century if you have schools that don't teach, a welfare system that destroys the family, a drug culture, and all the things we currently have.

So if you don't have a revolution, you're going to have a country which is decaying. And I think our goal is very simple. It is our goal to replace the welfare state. Not to reform it, not to improve it, not to modify it, to replace it. To go straight at the core structure and the core values of the welfare state, and replace them with a much more powerful, much more effective system.

**Remarks at the Young Republicans Leadership
Conference, Washington, D.C.
March 19, 1992**

Taking the streets back from violent crime and drugs, so that local TV news is no longer a death watch, would be a revolution in every major American city. Replacing welfare with workfare and ending a process by which teenage mothers have children outside marriage with ignorant, irresponsible male children who have sex but are not fathers would be a revolution. Having schools that are disciplined, require homework and beat the Japanese in math and science would be a revolution. Replacing the most expensive, red-tape-ridden litigious health care system in the world with a revitalized, health-oriented private system we can afford, and that would be available to everyone, would be a revolution. Having government bureaucracies that are lean, efficient, courteous and customer-service-oriented would be a revolution. Having a tax code that favored work, savings and investment, that helped create more and better jobs, greater productivity and higher take-home pay to make us the fastest-growing industrial economy in the world would be a revolution.

Congressional Record
January 3, 1992

29

The time has come to us to build a new model of American government that is more potent than the welfare state. . . .

The basic changes that I am proposing are simple:

from liberal	to conservative
from welfare	to opportunity
from the state	to the society at large.

WINDOW OF OPPORTUNITY, by Newt Gingrich with David Drake and Marianne Gingrich. A TOR Book, published by Tom Doherty Associates, Inc., New York City, in association with Baen Enterprises, Inc. 1984

In my opinion, the right direction for America's 21st century will involve a shift back toward traditional values and conservative basic principles such as work, thrift, and a strong criminal justice system.

WINDOW OF OPPORTUNITY

The 1990s must be a decade of invention, innovation, creativity and reform. We must decentralize power and programs away from Washington. We must liberate individuals, neighborhoods and local and state governments so they can experiment with new and better methods of getting the job done.

Heritage Lecture, "The Washington
Establishment vs. The American People:
A Report from the Budget Summit"
August 22, 1990

My statement of facts, obvious to every American outside of Washington, will prove how far out of touch Washington is, because if you use common sense and tell the truth in America, you are a radical in Washington.

Heritage Lecture, "The Washington
Establishment vs. The American People:
A Report from the Budget Summit"
August 22, 1990

I will not rest until I have transformed the landscape of American politics.

Los Angeles Times Magazine
August 25, 1991

4. THE SICK SOCIETY

No society can survive, no civilization can survive with 12-year-olds having babies, with 15-year-olds killing each other, with 17-year-olds dying of AIDS, with 18-year-olds getting diplomas they can't read.

Speech at the Capitol,
Washington, D.C.
December 5, 1994

Just as most Americans exceed the speed limit when they are driving, so the proliferation of red tape and bureaucracy leads to a proliferation of cheating. Ultimately, the burden will become too great and our society will resemble the decaying Ottoman Empire rather than the honest, open system we have known as the American Way.

WINDOW OF OPPORTUNITY

People like me are what stand between us and Auschwitz. I see evil all around me every day. . . .We are at the edge of losing this civilization. You get two more generations of what we had for the last 20 years and we're in desperate trouble. . . . As long as I believe that's true, I'll keep trying to recruit another generation and train another generation so that when I'm too tired to keep doing this, they'll be ready to step in. . . .

I don't want my country to collapse. I don't want my daughter and wife raped and killed. I don't want to see my neighborhood destroyed.

The Atlanta Constitution
January 17, 1994

The mother [Susan Smith] killing the two children in South Carolina vividly reminds every American how sick the society is getting and how much we need to change things. The only way you get change is to vote Republican.

Reuters
November 15, 1994

33

The Menendez trial now in California . . . is an absolutely fascinating example of the current cultural pathology. It's the newest version of the Twinkies defense: My parents abused me so much that as a young adult, I couldn't move out because I was so totally abused that I had to kill them, because after all, they might eventually have done something which would have made me feel bad. And it tells you how sick the culture is that the jury got hung. I mean, what do you need to know? The kids went in and blew away their parents.

Renewing American Civilization, Class 2

The traditional emphasis on work is under severe attack. The most obvious examples are the dropouts, the hippies, the people who use loopholes in the welfare system to draw unjustified benefits. However these often discussed (and attacked) examples are just the tip of the iceberg.

The real effort to get out of work in this century involves the average American. There has been constant pressure for shorter work weeks, larger vacations and earlier retirement.

"A Bicentennial Dialogue"
The Georgian **(Carrollton, Ga.)**
March 18, 1976

PART II
DYSFUNCTIONAL POLITICS

Gingrich's baptism by mire in three Georgia congressional races helped him to perfect his attack skills once he was finally elected to Congress. And attack he did, almost as soon as he reached the House floor. His stated purpose was to break the corrupt Democratic stranglehold on the House, and his strategy was twofold: to launch broadsides blaming society's ills on the influence of the "looney left" and the "Liberal Welfare State" as well as frontal attacks on Democratic figures for alleged character flaws or ethical violations.

With his take-no-prisoners rhetoric and carefully planned guerrilla warfare tactics, Gingrich's past behavior has evoked comparisons to Joseph McCarthy, the red-baiting senator who dominated the headlines in the early 1950s. Gingrich invariably branded Democrats as "left-wing" and frequently linked them to "socialism" and "communism." Speaker Jim Wright was called "pro-communist." New York Governor Mario Cuomo was lambasted for being "the most articulate spokesman of the pre-perestroika, Brezhnev wing of the Democratic Party." Democratic candidates Bill Clinton and Al Gore had a "pre-Gorbachev, centralized-bureaucracy vision." Other Democrats were associated with criminals—"thugs," "muggers" or cheats in Gingrich's lexicon. At the Republican National Convention in 1992, Gingrich impugned the patriotism of the Democratic Party, charging that it "rejects the lessons of American history, despises the values of the American people and denies the basic goodness of the American nation."

Even though he first ran for Congress in a district carried by one-time segregationist George Wallace in an unsuccessful presidential quest, Gingrich has generally refrained from using racial issues to his advantage. While some of his comments about welfare state victims are tinged with racial undertones, most of the time he sincerely emphasizes the need to recognize that America is a multiethnic and multicultural society. He argues that the GOP can no longer afford to be "the party of the country clubs" and instead has to evolve into a party "that cares enough about the poor to actually help them, rather than a party that cares just enough about them to exploit them."

The news media, along with the intellectual elite government bureaucrats and liberals of every size and description, have been easy targets for Gingrich's verbal firebombs, but his relationship with the Fourth Estate in fact has been symbiotic. Gingrich and a small band of conservative legislators first got exposure for their views in the early '80s by taking advantage of House of Representatives "special minutes" and "special orders" allowing members to speak uninterrupted on the topic of their choice. It didn't matter that the House chamber was usually deserted, about the same time, C-Span initiated uninterrupted coverage of the House's proceedings giving Gingrich and his colleagues a national audience. Besides, Gingrich frankly acknowledges that much of his behavior as a backbencher was geared toward attracting press coverage.

As Minority Whip, Gingrich continued to find inventive ways to disseminate his views. His recent lectures on "Renewing American Civilization" were videotaped at Reinhardt College in Waleska, Georgia, and subsequently broadcast by satellite over the National Empowerment Television network and taught for credit at as many as 25 universities. Newt Gingrich may have a healthy contempt for the news media, but he has been shrewder than any contemporary politician in knowing how to manipulate media to serve his pedagogic and political purposes.

5. THE REPUBLICANS

The Republican Party is in real danger of dying. The bunting and the banners around us could well be the flowers at our party's funeral.

Speech, "The Survival of the Two-Party System"
(Ingram Library, West Georgia College)
1976

In my lifetime—literally in my lifetime, I was born in 1943—we have not had a competent national Republican leader. Not ever!

Speech to College Republicans in Atlanta
June 24, 1978

For the last 50 years the Republican Party has been hypnotized by Franklin Roosevelt, and its entire vision has been to stop what he began.

As quoted in *Changing of the Guard*, by David Broder.
Simon & Schuster, New York City
1980

The great Republican tradition which my family identified with . . . was the 1856-to-1912 tradition that was very progressive. It was the party of industrialization, of economic growth. It was the party of the full lunch pail. And that party was very activist. That was the party that created the land-grant colleges and built the transcontinental railroad. It had a vision which it was willing to impose upon the society. . . .

So I'm a modernizer who is suggesting that we leap back an entire span and claim our own heritage again.

**As quoted in *Changing of the Guard,*
by David Broder**

The fact is, every Republican has much to learn from studying what the Democrats did right.

The New York Times
January 5, 1995

I am a Republican, but I think the greatest failure of the last 20 years has been the Republican Party, not the Democratic Party. The Democratic Party has attempted to do what the governing party should do—govern. But it failed. And when it failed, there was nobody there to take up the burden. And I think that in order for this civilization to survive, at least as a free society, we've got to have a more rigorous and cohesive sense of an alternative party.

As quoted in *Changing of the Guard,*
by David Broder

If the Democrats have to rethink their strategy after losing five out of six presidential races, shouldn't Republicans do some thinking about why they have lost 18 consecutive elections for a majority in the House?

Comments at Heritage Foundation symposium,
"Is George Bush Mr. Right?"
Policy Review
Winter 1989

The Republican Party remains an inadequate instrument for serving the vast majority of Americans who have rejected the Left. . . . The Democrats' forces include the AFL-CIO, the NAACP, big city governments, the Legal Services Corporation, the tax-paid advantages of incumbency, and the capacity of congressional committee chairmen to coerce PACs into giving money to Democrats. The Republican Party is incapable of competing with the Left's organizational strength and professionalism.

Comments at Heritage Foundation symposium,
"Is George Bush Mr. Right?"
Policy Review
Winter 1989

Historically, the Democrats were the party of the cities and the party of the poor and the party of minorities. . . . Historically, Republicans were seen as the party of the country clubs. What we have to become is a party that cares enough about the poor to actually help them, rather than a party that cares just enough about them to exploit them. It has to change by our being, not just by our speaking.

The Atlanta Journal-Constitution
June 9, 1991

6. THE CONSERVATIVE MOVEMENT

The only hope we have to build an effective conservative majority is to use the Republican Party as our vehicle. I do not suggest that it is an ideal choice. The last two campaigns have proven to me personally that I run each time with a 700-pound elephant on my back as a handicap.

> Fund-raising dinner, Hospitality Inn,
> Atlanta, Georgia
> October 29, 1977

Conservatism makes no sense as a short-term value system. The conservative issue is life for your grandchildren.

> Comments at Heritage Foundation symposium,
> "What Conservatives Think of
> Ronald Reagan"
> *Policy Review*
> Winter 1984

The Republican Party has to be the conservative party if it is to mobilize the 61 per cent of the country which calls itself more conservative than liberal. However, this conservatism has to be moderate if the party is not to be isolated from the bulk of the population, which rejects either extreme. Conservatism also has to be defined in a populist manner which can attract the blue-collar workers who are suspicious of Republican ties to big business. The party must consciously remain conservative while being willing to challenge the group which Gallup has reported is the least trusted segment in America—big business beat out both big labor and big government.

Comments at Heritage Foundation symposium,
"Is George Bush Mr. Right?"
Policy Review
Winter 1989

The real challenge to the conservative movement, and this is very different than complaining about or being opposed to government, is to figure out the combination of voluntary and government replacements which . . . would replace the welfare state.

The Washington Times
March 6, 1991

7. THE DEMOCRATS

They [Georgia Democratic Party leaders] are pleasant people who behind the scenes are thugs.

The Atlanta Journal
May 20, 1989

The pompous politicians who lead this majority party are the Pharisees. They stand in the doorway refusing to enter themselves, but blocking the pathway of anyone else who might wish to do so.

Speech to 6th District Republican
Training Session in Carrollton, Georgia
(Ingram Library, West Georgia College)
November 8, 1975

It used to be called socialism. It is now just sort of liberal Democratic platform pledges.

Congressional Record
August 2, 1984

Michael Dukakis has never in his life been out of the United States on a business trip. He never went overseas to deal with heads of state. . . .

[He] dislikes the military so much that for 10 years he has declined invitations to visit the largest Air Force base in Massachusetts.

So you have a man . . . who is utterly ignorant of the world and utterly ignorant of military affairs, and this is the guy we're going to put next to the nuclear button?

I would just ask you to think about that and just ask yourself, how much do we know about this guy? How big a risk would having him in the White House be?

Comments after Dukakis, then governor of Massachusetts, was nominated for president at the Democratic Convention in Atlanta.
The Atlanta Constitution
July 31, 1988

It's going to be a Dukakis–[Jesse] Jackson administration no matter who the vice presidential nominee is. It's really hard to imagine how far left-wing these people are.

For example, Gov. Dukakis favors letting prisoners out on the weekend. . . . I've even been told that Dukakis' staff is in the prisons registering prisoners to vote so they can help defeat a referendum that would stop prisoners from getting out on weekends. I think the average Georgian would think this is nuts. I mean, this is not us.

The Rome (Ga.) Christian News
April 1988

The reports I've seen indicate that his wife [Kitty Dukakis] was a drug addict for 27 years, on diet pills. Dukakis' answer when asked about it was, he had not noticed.

The Atlanta Constitution
July 31, 1988

He [opponent Dennis Worley] is the least ethical candidate I have ever had to run against. He's a Harvard magna cum laude graduate; he's very smart, proof that IQ and honor are not always the same thing. This man is so despicable and so desperate to be a congressman that he is deliberately scaring 80- and 90-year-old people with what he knows is a lie. ·

Commenting on Worley's allegations that Gingrich's aim is to abolish the social security system.
The Atlanta Journal-Constitution
July 28, 1988

Conservatives should systematically desert the Democratic Party as long as it remains a left-wing party. They should force the Democratic Party into the kind of bankruptcy that Margaret Thatcher forced on the Labor Party in Britain.

Comments at Heritage Foundation symposium, "Is George Bush Mr. Right?"
Policy Review
Winter 1989

48

The Democrats in the [Capitol] building get up every morning knowing that to survive they need do only two things: They lie regularly and they cheat.

The Washington Times
May 19, 1989

"a trio of muggers"

Characterization of Democratic House leaders
Jim Wright, Tip O'Neill and Tom Foley.
As quoted in *The Washington Post*
June 12, 1989

"a left-wing lynch mob"

Characterization of Democrat-led
Iran-Contra hearings.
As quoted in *The Washington Post*
June 12, 1989

"pro-communist"

Description of Democratic House Speaker
Jim Wright at the time he tried to
negotiate with Nicaragua's Sandinista-
led government.
As quoted in *The Washington Post*
June 12, 1989

[Mario Cuomo is] the most articulate spokesman of the pre-perestroika, Brezhnev wing of the Democratic Party. . . . his defeat would put to rest the claim that liberalism could win in America if only it wasn't represented by such incompetent campaigners as Mondale and Dukakis.

The New York Times
July 19, 1990

Imagine, the party of [Joseph] Biden, [Charles] Robb and [Edward] Kennedy talking about experience.

**Commenting on three prominent Democrats at
the time the Senate Judiciary Committee
was reviewing Clarence Thomas' nomination
to the Supreme Court.
As recorded in *The Boston Globe*
August 11, 1991**

I call this the Woody Allen plank. It's a weird situation, and it fits the Democratic Party platform perfectly. If a Democrat used the word "family" to raise children in Madison Square Garden, half their party would have rebelled, and the other half would not vote. Woody Allen had non-incest with his non-daughter because they were a non-family.

Commenting on the 1992 Democratic platform adopted at the National Convention in New York City.
The Washington Post
August 26, 1992

[In Al Gore's book *Earth in the Balance*] there's a paragraph where, having explained dysfunctionality for about six pages, he then explains the worst—he describes this terrible century as compared to Reagan's vision of the American century. He then compares the U.S. to a dysfunctional civilization. . . . Astroturf, plastic flowers, air conditioning and frozen foods from microwave ovens. I mean, it is just the sort of nutty left-wing goo-goo stuff.

Unpublished interview with *U.S. News & World Report* at Republican Convention in Houston
August 19, 1992

[Bill Clinton] is a very smart, very clever tactician whose core system of activity is a combination of counterculture and McGovern. He was McGovern's Texas director, he and his wife were counterculture at Yale, and why wouldn't you accept that they really are who they are? Their problem is, that is a contradiction with the vast majority of Americans. So you have this constant internal stress and what the American people were saying is "Enough."

The New York Times
November 10, 1994

We are looking for a dacha. We think Leon and George need dachas.

Recommending retirement for Leon Panetta,
White House Chief of Staff, and George
Stephanopoulos, assistant to the President.
The Washington Post
October 25, 1994

I think that for many of our good friends who happen to be liberal Democrats, this is the end of an age. The liberal welfare state is dying, their values are collapsing, public support for their deepest beliefs is waning. In a sense, someone may one day write a book entitled *The Waning of the Liberal Welfare State* and look at this period and say that in 1980 the American people rejected the basic tenets of the liberal welfare state. In that sense, this is a time of great sadness for the Speaker of the House, for many other liberal Democrats who spent a lifetime building a structure which they see crumbling before their very eyes.

Congressional Record
April 1, 1982

8. THE LOONEY LEFT

The term "looney left" was developed by Margaret Thatcher and the Conservative Party in Britain to describe people whose views were so weird, so far out of touch with reality, so unusual that no other term was good enough.

Congressional Record
April 28, 1988

The Record of today's debates and votes [on defense spending] should be instructive to every American. Today offered proof that a Democratic machine runs the U.S. House of Representatives. That machine caters to and is dominated by its looney left, and it is willing to change the rules of the House on a daily basis to ensure that it sets the agenda, it decides what issues can be voted on and under what circumstances each vote will occur.

Congressional Record
April 28, 1988

The looney left intimidates and frightens the senior Democrats and the committee and sub-committee chairmen by threatening to strip them of their chairmanships if they vote against the looney left on foreign and defense matters.

Congressional Record
April 28, 1988

One of the tragedies of the last 20 years has been the fact that the Liberalism which gives the most speeches about jobs has done more than any other element of our society to kill jobs.

WINDOW OF OPPORTUNITY

The cultural attitudes of the left and the counter-culture are so anti-technology that they are slowing down the development of new medicines, the development of new learning systems and, in general, the development of new ways of getting things done.

Introduction by Newt Gingrich,
in *Readings in Renewing American Civilization,*
**edited by Jeffrey A. Eisenach and Albert Stephen
Hanser. McGraw-Hill, Inc., New York City,
1993**

The values of the Left cripple human beings, weaken cities, make it difficult for us to in fact survive as a country. . . . The Left in America is to blame for most of the current, major diseases which have struck this society.

Mother Jones
October 1989

Because the Left has rejected any hope of salvation through technological innovation, Liberals led the fight against building the space shuttle in the early 1970s. Their argument was that research and development money was wasted because it had no immediate impact on Earth, while more money for food stamps was good because it provided an immediate benefit. This school of thought, which demands immediate gratification because it holds that there is no future, has gained force in the last decade.

WINDOW OF OPPORTUNITY

There's only a very small counterculture elite, which is terrified of the opportunity to actually renew American civilization.

The New York Times
November 10, 1994

The whole Clinton campaign strategy has to be to obscure their allies and to obscure their promises until they get to the election, because if the American people read the fine print, we are not in bad enough economic shape that if you take the combination of inflation and unemployment, we are not in bad enough shape for this country to go to a relatively strong left-wing position. And if you read Clinton's promises, they're frankly fairly left-wing. I mean, what's more left-wing than his style?

Unpublished interview with *U.S. News & World Report* at Republican Convention in Houston
August 19, 1992

9. THE INTELLECTUAL ELITE

[Sinclair Lewis's] Babbitt's grandson, now a Ph.D. in Sociology, earns a pittance, lives in genteel poverty, drives an old Volvo. . . . He feels morally superior to his high school classmates who entered business, medicine and law: they earn more than he does, but he *knows* more. . . . The left-wing ideological biases of the academic community are now as much a barrier to truth as were the right-wing biases of the business community in the 1920s.

WINDOW OF OPPORTUNITY

. . . it is essential to understand why *The Killing Fields* had rave reviews from left-wing intellectuals, while *Rambo* was laughed at. *Rambo* was overtly anti-Communist, while *The Killing Fields* managed to somehow pin the blame on America for what was clearly a Communist genocidal action in Cambodia.

Congressional Record
March 21, 1986

Either we recapture universities for Western values, and make them once again useful, or they will become what English universities once were—quaint artifacts where youths go to listen to weird people tell them bizarre things, none of which are real.

The Boston Globe
August 11, 1991

I hope the next three Democratic presidential campaigns are run by people conversant with the Kennedy School. Only the Stanford Faculty have been more aggressive in trying to prove they can be more out of touch with the American people than the Kennedy School.

The Boston Globe
August 11, 1991

Mussolini, Stalin and Hitler would have admired some of the elite campuses where certain words can get a student expelled.

The Boston Globe
August 11, 1991

10. THE ANTI-DEISTS AND THE "CULTURAL WAR"

My vision is of an America that realizes that its real strength is spiritual, not economic. Our deepest need is for leaders who have a commitment to morality above winning. Above all, we need leaders who bring their private sense of right and wrong into the public arena.

Speech announcing candidacy for Congress
(Ingram Library, West Georgia College)
March 22, 1976

Despite attempts by today's anti-deists to abolish God and religion in public life, it is impossible to study the leaders of the American Revolution without being profoundly impressed by their commitment to God and to divining His will. Even our most radical founding father, Thomas Jefferson, wrote in the Declaration of

Independence that all men are "endowed by their Creator with certain unalienable rights." Thus the very first document by which we proclaimed our freedom from British hegemony asserted that this freedom was granted to us by God and not man.

WINDOW OF OPPORTUNITY

Now, it does strike me as slightly strange that this man [Thomas Jefferson] who all of my liberal friends assure did not believe in God, decided that it was on God's altar that he would swear eternal hostility. But I'm sure that was probably just a little PR trick of that period.

Referring to Jefferson's words inscribed on the
ceiling of the Jefferson Memorial: "I have sworn
upon the altar of God eternal hostility against
every form of tyranny over the mind of man."
Remarks to a group of state legislators
December 1994

I had a very bright student in the class who said, "Well, do you really think voluntary school prayer matters that much?" And I suddenly realized that I really did think it mattered that much, that I think we are crazy to have driven it out.

Renewing American Civilization, Class 2

. . . our liberal national elite doesn't believe in religion.

Mother Jones
1984

For a generation, the values which were written into the Declaration of Independence . . . have been eroding; we have carried money saying "In God We Trust," while politicians and the ACLU have driven God out of our public life and institutions.

WINDOW OF OPPORTUNITY

Our intelligentsia and news media will find
it easier to believe in lunar bases and super computers than to consider the possibility that spiritual and moral issues may be re-emerging as a
central theme in American life.

WINDOW OF OPPORTUNITY

You have absolutely in the abstract a cultural civil war going on. I've said this for—all you
have heard me say this before. I wouldn't use
the wars of religion—only to the degree that a
nihilistic hedonism and secular belief pattern is
by definition involved in a religious war with a
spiritual system. I mean, intellectually, if you're
writing a history of the 20th century, you could
write that out.

Unpublished interview with U.S. News & World
Report at Republican Convention in Houston
August 19, 1992

11. THE NEWS MEDIA

Since I was nine, I've been oriented toward facilitating the media.

> **Commenting on his newspaper article asking the mayor of Harrisburg, Pa., to establish a local zoo. Shortly afterward, he was able to wangle five minutes weekly on TV to talk about the exotic offerings from a local pet shop.**
> *Los Angeles Times*
> **August 5, 1991**

I'm a controversial guy. . . . [I'm] reshaping the entire nation through the news media.

> *Vanity Fair*
> **July 1989**

C-Span is more real than being there.

> *The Atlanta Constitution*
> **February 7, 1985**

The number one fact about the news media is they love fights. . . . the minute Tip O'Neill attacked me [for speaking before an empty House chamber and challenging the Democrats to respond], he and I got 90 seconds at the close of all three network news shows. You have to give them confrontations. When you give them confrontations, you get attention; when you get attention, you can educate.

Comment after Speaker of the House
Thomas O'Neill lambasted him for
his behavior on the House floor.
Mother Jones
November 1984

As an elected official, I can hold a press conference and that's a source of real power. . . . The ambitions that this city focuses on are trivial if you're a historian. Who cares?

The Washington Post
January 3, 1985

If you're not in *The Washington Post* every day, you might as well not exist.

Vanity Fair
July 1989

News media coverage is frankly sometimes distorted, but more often it is simply uninformed or unfocused. All too often the new ideas, the new terms, the new leaders, are outside the cocktail party circuit of the liberal news media.

Congressional Record
April 5, 1982

People are not in general stupid, but they are often ignorant. In their ignorance they often tolerate ignorant news reporters who in turn tolerate ignorant politicians. The result is an ignorant politician making an ignorant speech to be covered by an ignorant reporter and shown in a 40-second clip on television to an ignorant audience.

Window of Opportunity

Now, when you deal with [media] people, you have to remember two things: absolute certainty and knowledge of detail. That's what these reporters and editors want.

The Atlantic Monthly
May 1985

Why don't you do this? Why don't you write a letter to Meg Greenfield [editorial-page editor of *The Washington Post*]? Say, "I'm a freshman, I'm a presidential scholar, Tony Coelho [House Democratic Whip] is engaged in an explicit campaign of disinformation, and I don't know what the procedure is for sitting down with your editorial board." Send it to Ms. Meg Greenfield. And put a P.S. on it that says, "Newt Gingrich told me that sometimes idealism really works." And after a few weeks of this at least she'll return your phone calls. At least she'll know who Joe Barton is. And then you'll be influencing *The Washington Post*. Okay? Take care.

**Advice in a telephone conversation
to Congressman Joe Barton,
as reported in
The Atlantic Monthly
May 1985**

TV news directors [are] *real* important. Incredibly important. That's the central nervous system. They're the ones who make the decision to put Gingrich on. If we can do *Face the Nation,* that's *very* valuable. I mean, last night's dinner [at the National Press Club] made no sense, except the news media could see me walking through the crowd. I still can't get used to the idea that so many people want me to come to the dance.

The Atlantic Monthly
May 1985

I've done very few things that were hip shots in my career. The style of being aggressive enough and different enough when you guys cover me is conscious.

The Atlantic Monthly
June 1993

12. WHAT'S WRONG WITH CONGRESS

Congress is a sicker and sicker institution in an imperial capital that wallows in the American people's tax money.

August 1990 speech, as quoted in
The Wall Street Journal
September 17, 1990

We can elect conservative Presidents for the rest of this century and as long as they are facing liberal Congresses there will be no change. . . . In the United States Constitution they [the Founding Fathers] actually placed the Congress in Article One as the first or preeminent branch of government.

Speech at Republican District Convention
in Jonesboro, Georgia
May 22, 1976

The world is just too complex now to have randomly chosen president-kings who may or may not be competent.

As quoted in *Changing of the Guard,*
by David Broder

Democrats would go on the floor to kick Republicans and show their contempt. The ranking Republicans would say how grateful they were to work with the Chairman, when he had 70 staff people and the Republican had three. It was the whole psychology of master and servant.

Recalling the treatment of Republicans
during his early years in Congress.
The Washington Post
August 26, 1984

[When] Ronald Reagan's steak goes into a liberal welfare state triangle, it comes out as hamburger. No matter how good the idea was to begin with, by the time the special interests of the liberal welfare state get done tearing it apart, by the time they get done exposing every detail, by the time they slant their questions and their code words, it ends up being torn to shreds.

Congressional Record
April 5, 1982

In 1989, you were 16 times as likely to be defeated if you were a Soviet provincial Communist leader than if you were a member of the U.S. House of Representatives.

One out of every three Soviet provincial leaders was defeated. . . . The fact is that for the first time in 200 years we have a political machine dominating the Capitol in such a way that it is literally preventing free elections.

The Washington Times
May 19, 1989

13. GOVERNMENT BUREAUCRACY

I believe in a lean bureaucracy, not in no bureaucracy. You can have an active, aggressive, conservative state which does not in fact have a large centralized bureaucracy. . . . This goes back to Teddy Roosevelt. We have not seen an *activist* conservative presidency since TR.

Mother Jones
November 1984

Bureaucracy teaches that process is more important than achievement, that red tape is more important than productivity, and bureaucrats dominate productive people. So the bureaucrat defines reality.

Renewing American Civilization, Class 3

We are also facing an increasing crisis in the morale and competence of our civil service. As workers see their office equipment and prestige decay, they lose self-respect and professional pride. Budget crunches lead to smaller or even no pay raises; pension reform takes away some of their past benefits; and political speeches denigrate their worth. Morale and daily performance suffer accordingly. . . . A great nation cannot remain great if its central governing agencies are demoralized, incompetent, and ineffective.

WINDOW OF OPPORTUNITY

You can walk into a Wal-Mart store today and have your credit card approved in 2.3 seconds. And yet it takes the Veterans Department six weeks to answer your letter. We Republicans see the efficiency of Wal-Mart and of UPS; we want to change government to be as courteous, efficient, speedy and effective as those companies. The Democrats see those companies, and they want to apply litigation, regulation and taxation to make sure the companies become more like government.

Speech, Republican National Convention in Houston
August 18, 1992

If the federal government had improved in efficiency as much as the computer has since 1950, we'd only need four federal employees and the federal budget would be $100,000.

Renewing American Civilization, Class 4

We have to engage in a deep, thorough dialogue with the American people on how to shrink the federal government to achieve a balance. We cannot replace the social engineering by the left with a social engineering of the right.

**Heritage Lecture, "What the Elections
Mean to Conservatives"
November 15, 1994**

14. POLITICAL STRATEGY

One of the great problems we have in the Republican Party is that we don't encourage you to be nasty. We encourage you to be neat, obedient, and loyal and faithful, and all those Boy Scout words, which would be great around the camp fire, but are lousy in politics.

Speech to College Republicans in Atlanta
June 24, 1978

Don't try to educate them [the voters]; that is not your job. You're in the politics business.

Speech to College Republicans in Atlanta
June 24, 1978

It is time that we learn to talk the language of the average American. Most people in this country do not talk about energy crises. They talk about the price of gasoline. Most Americans do not listen to Secretary of Agriculture [Earl] Butz's complex reassurances about selling wheat to the Russians; they worry about the price of bread. Balanced budgets are distant and complicated ideas, while Medicare and decent housing are immediate and understandable. . . .

Frankly, Republicans preach too much and listen too little. That is one reason we have such a small flock.

Speech, "The Survival of the Two-Party System"
(Ingram Library, West Georgia College)
1976

You do not want to elect politicians who say "trust me," 'cause you can't trust anybody, not just politicians.

Speech to College Republicans in Atlanta
June 24, 1978

We Republicans must take four steps to develop our strength for the upcoming election. First, we must talk honestly and without fear about the history of our times and the issues which dominate. Second, we must recognize that we are involved in politics and not merely a debating society. Third, we must develop our role as the party of the middle-class working tax-payers; these are the common sense conservatives who are the overwhelming majority of Americans. Fourth, we must practice evangelism and pursue every voter.

Speech, "The Survival of the Two-Party System"
(Ingram Library, West Georgia College)
1976

We have eager, enthusiastic, decent, hard-working players suiting up for soccer while we are engaged in a professional football game.

Memo to President Bush,
"Key Principles for a Successful 1992,"
dated February 28, 1992.
Published in *The Washington Post*
March 12, 1992

[President Bush] has to make sure people understand that the Democrats have held the House since Bill Clinton was in the second grade.

Unpublished interview with *U.S. News & World Report* at Republican Convention in Houston
August 19, 1992

Now, there are two salient facts about our next choice. . . . Fact No. 1 is for four years he's [President Bush] gone to a pharmacy controlled by Democrats, and the Democrats have given him either no medicine or they've given him bad medicine. Fact No. 2, the alternative doctors in town, Dr. Feelgood and Dr. Smilegood, are nice young guys, [they] have a terrific guaranteed quick diet plan, 28-pound weight loss. The problem is, when you read the fine print, they get to the weight loss by amputating your leg. And the question is: Am I really eager enough to have a change that I'll risk having my leg amputated?

Unpublished interview with *U.S. News & World Report* at Republican Convention in Houston
August 19, 1992

15. HEROES AND VILLAINS

My life was changed three layers by Lincoln. First, as I said earlier, when I would lose. . . . I've lost it now—but I used to carry a little clipping about Lincoln's defeats that was given to me when I was 13 by a weekly newspaper editor who said, "It takes perseverance. Never give up." . . . Second, in reading things like [Carl] Sandburg's great biography of Lincoln. . . . And then in recent years, I had gotten about seven years ago very tired, and I'd been doing—I'd been involved in public life and I was sort of worn down, and I picked up a book by [Stephen] Oates, which is a biography of Lincoln. Oates is a modern romantic, probably fairly liberal, a guy who may be shocked to know that he had changed my life. But he understood that Lincoln was about you. Lincoln understood that what America was was an experiment in the idea that each individual person was as important as the king.

Renewing American Civilization, Class 6

If you truly love democracy and you truly believe in representative self-government, you can never study Franklin Delano Roosevelt too much. He did bring us out of the Depression. He did lead the allied movement in World War II. In many ways he created the modern world. He was clearly, I think, as a political leader the greatest figure of the 20th century. And I think his concept that we have nothing to fear but fear itself, that we'll take an experiment, and if it fails, we'll do another one, and if you go back and read the New Deal, they tried again and again. They didn't always get it right, and we would have voted against much of it, but the truth is we would have voted for much of it.

**Speech at the Capitol,
Washington, D.C.
December 5, 1994**

I'd like to have Eisenhower's humanness.
. . . One of the reasons I keep reading Eisenhower is that he was very successful at getting along with people who despised him.

The Washington Post
January 3, 1985

[Hubert Humphrey was] a spellbinder on the stump [but] he has not had a new idea since 1948.

Speech to 6th District Republican
Training Session in Carrollton, Georgia
(Ingram Library, West Georgia College)
November 8, 1975

President Kennedy knew high taxes were putting people out of work. Taxes got so high people couldn't afford to buy much of anything. Companies couldn't sell their products, so people got laid off and other people never got hired.

Campaign flyer
(Ingram Library, West Georgia College)
1978

In 1960 I worked very hard in Columbus [Georgia] for the Nixon/Lodge ticket. One of the longest nights of my life was that election when, as a high school senior, I listened on radio to the Chicago and Texas Democratic machines stealing the election. That bitter pill became even more bitter 14 years later when the people who had profited from their own theft in 1960 became pious and served as judges in Congress on the man they had stolen from.

Speech, "The Survival of the Two-Party System"
(Ingram Library, West Georgia College)
1976

In my lifetime, without question, the President who lied the most and did the most damage to the United States was Lyndon Johnson. It was Johnson who misled the American people about war in Asia. It was Johnson who designed a disastrous economic policy that fueled the inflation from which we are only now recovering. It was Johnson's politics of irresponsible promises which led to riots on the campuses and in the cities. It is Johnson's "Great

Society" which is smothering us in red tape, fiscal deficits, and massive bureaucracy.

Speech, "The Survival of the Two-Party System"
(Ingram Library, West Georgia College)
1976

Carter is a conservative when he smiles, a moderate liberal when he talks, and a Mc-Govern-Humphrey liberal when he issues detailed position papers. Carter's governorship reorganized itself into bigger and bigger government. He was and is pro-welfare, pro-bureaucracy and pro-deficit spending.

Remarks at the 6th Republican
District Convention, Jonesboro, Georgia
May 22, 1976

Somebody who is a personal example of this sustained citizenship and this commitment to community, somebody you wouldn't normally expect me maybe to be as positive about as I am, is Jimmy Carter, who . . . I think is one of the two best former presidents we've ever had, the other one being John Quincy Adams, who went back and served in the Congress for, I think, 14 years.

Renewing American Civilization, Class 10

About half-way to Atlanta, the President [Reagan] came back to where I was sitting. We spent about 35 minutes talking about the problems of communicating with the Washington press corps and the frustrations he faced in his job.

It was interesting to me as a third term Member of Congress to listen to a man who could reminisce about his experiences in the 1940s in fighting Communism in the movie industry, and the lessons he had learned the hard way as the head of a union while negotiating with the movie industry.

Commenting on his trip on *Air Force One*.
He had made a special trip to Atlanta so
he could fly back with the President.
Newsletter to constituents
(Papers of David Worley)
August 5, 1983

. . . we stand on Ronald Reagan's shoulders.
. . . His ideas, his spirit, his optimism, his personality have shaped the modern Republican Party, defeated the Soviet empire, and extended freedom across the planet in a way that is truly historic.

Speech at the Capitol,
Washington, D.C.
December 5, 1994

Somebody once said that they thought [Charles] De Gaulle of all the modern figures could think the longest about something other than himself, until they realized that what he thought about was France, and that he thought France was himself. Therefore, he had simply redefined himself.

Renewing American Civilization, Class 3

I do not think Jane Fonda is any more reliable an expert on nuclear power than she was a patriot to North Vietnam. I think she is a great actress and I enjoy watching her but I have no more interest in her expertise in foreign policy, which is zill [sic], as I would in seeing Edward Kennedy as an actor.

Rural Georgia Magazine
December 1979

[David Stockman was] the greatest obstacle to a successful revolution from the Liberal Welfare State to an Opportunity Society.

The Atlantic Monthly
May 1985

I think, based on the historical record, he is the most unethical speaker of the 20th century.

Commenting on Jim Wright.
Associated Press
December 16, 1987

As a human I've always felt sympathy for him [Jim Wright]. I can feel sympathy for Willie Horton for being in jail for the rest of his life.

The New York Times
May 1, 1989

[Senator Bob Dole is] the tax collector of the welfare state.

The Washington Post
November 19, 1984

An older man of great experience. . . . I think Bob Dole is a tremendous leader. . . . I have never seen a more disciplined, energetic personality than Bob Dole.

1994 victory speech
in Marietta, Georgia
November 8, 1994

We [Gingrich and Bob Dole] are the most integrated House-Senate team in modern times.

The Wall Street Journal
November 9, 1994

Reagan says with humor what [Pat] Buchanan says with anger. . . . I think Buchanan is almost by definition a polarizer. Reagan accepts sadly the polarization you force on him, but he does accept it. And "evil empire" he knew would be a polarizing phrase. And Reagan was quite clever in the Napoleonic sense of a strategic offense and a tactical defense. He would lunge out here somewhere and then be unbelievably pleasant while people screamed at him. Buchanan's technique is to wade into the middle of a barroom brawl.

Unpublished interview with *U.S. News & World Report* at Republican Convention in Houston
August 19, 1992

[To compare Bush and Clinton,] the line I've been using is to decide you're irritated with Bush on taxes and decide to marry Clinton is like having dated a social drinker and ended up marrying a bartender. Bush may have some weaknesses on the tax side, but compared to Clinton he's almost—you know.

Unpublished interview with *U.S. News & World Report* at Republican Convention in Houston
August 19, 1992

[President Clinton is] the enemy of normal Americans.

The Washington Post
October 20, 1994

Leon Panetta in 1985 stole a seat from the people of Indiana. . . . Because at the last minute, he refused to count the last 23 votes because [former Democratic Whip] Tony Coelho had instructed him to steal the seat. That's how I feel about anything Leon Panetta says: a man who will steal a congressional seat from the people of Indiana will say anything.

Panetta was a member of a bipartisan task force to resolve a disputed House race in Indiana's 8th Congressional District in the 1984 election. The task force declared the Democrat the victor.
The Washington Post
October 25, 1994

Leon [Panetta] and I can work together. He's a competent person.

The Washington Post
October 25, 1994

There got to be a point during the budget summit that I was beginning to listen carefully to liberal Democratic arguments and tried to figure out how I could agree with them. When I got home I realized, in fact, that that was not why I got hired. I suddenly realized how real the "Stockholm Syndrome" is—when you are captured by a terrorist and start identifying with the kidnappers.

Commenting on working with the Democrats.
The New York Times
July 19, 1990

. . . look at the preachments of the Surgeon General [Joycelyn Elders] and ask yourself how could a President have a surgeon general who has suggested we consider legalizing drugs, who said at one point that she didn't see that selling cocaine was necessarily an illegal act, who has basically taken positions that are not just anti-Catholic but they, in effect, represent an attitude towards permissive sexuality that by any reasonable standard in a middle-class sense is destructive, and ask yourself why does the President keep her? I assume he shares her values. I assume he thinks it's okay.

Elders was fired by President Clinton a few days later when comments she made at a UN conference about masturbation were about to be reported.
Meet the Press
December 4, 1994

PART III
BRAVE NEW WORLDS

It's revealing that when Newt Gingrich has chosen his literary collaborators, whether it be nonfiction or fiction works, he has settled on (apart from his current wife) science fiction writers. "Newt's a big science fiction fan," one colleague once remarked. Among his advisers, too, have been a veritable constellation of visionaries and futurists—Alvin and Heidi Toffler (*Future Shock* and *The Third Wave*), renowned science fiction master Isaac Asimov, Herman Kahn, Peter Drucker and Edwards Deming, the business consultant behind the "quality" movement. Gingrich calls himself "a conservative futurist."

Gingrich's defining opus, so far, is *Window of Opportunity*, published in 1984.

The book, along with the 20-hour-long series of lectures entitled Renewing American Civilization, presents the most textured explanation of Gingrich's views— far more than the sound bites that make it onto the evening news. One striking note about both the book and the lectures, separated by a decade, is how little Gingrich's views have changed. Like many self-help gurus, Gingrich has no compunction about repeating himself. He'll open many of his lectures the same way. Similar, if not identical, passages find themselves in many of his political speeches. Many politicians, of course, have a standard stump speech, but few have stuck with the same basic text for so long.

Gingrich's vision of the future is profoundly optimistic—if Americans choose the correct path. In *Window of Opportunity*, written at the time he was chairman of the Congressional Space Caucus, Gingrich was confident that many of Earth's intractable problems could be solved by extraterrestrial development. Not only would there be Marriots and Hiltons in space, but there would also be vast possibilities for manufacturing profitable new products. Space exploration would promote cooperation among terrestrial nations and provide jobs for the handicapped, who would be able to take advantage of the no-gravity work environment.

Gingrich's recent enthusiasms have been more down-to-earth: new information technologies and the rise of global markets are the powerful forces transforming our society. Gingrich was stalwart in his support of the North American Free Trade Agreement (NAFTA) as well as the new General Agreement on Tariffs and Trade (GATT), although in both cases it meant making common cause with the Clinton administration and many Democrats. His faith in new technologies is seemingly limitless and almost childlike. The "Third Wave" information revolution—Gingrich borrows the term from the Tofflers—will allow us to carry a device "slightly larger than your wristwatch" with "a capacity to interact electronically worldwide in real time." Other revolutionary technologies will let us work at home, freeing us to "schedule that birthday party or Cub Scout meeting which used to be so troublesome." A "health chair" will monitor our diet and bodily symptoms. If society provides a large monetary incentive, he asserts, entrepreneurs will be motivated to discover a miracle cure for kidney disease and other ailments.

To Gingrich, the future holds endless possibility; paraphrasing Ronald Reagan's slogan, it is, once again, morning in Middle America. As for the details, they are a little sketchy, but as long as the philosophy and principles are right, Gingrich believes, the details will take care of themselves.

16. WINDOW OF OPPORTUNITY

In Franklin Delano Roosevelt's words, "Our generation has a rendezvous with destiny."

Congressional Record
January 25, 1993

There exists for the United States today a window of opportunity through which we can look, and—with luck and hard work—reach to create a bright and optimistic future for our children and grandchildren. If, however, we continue the policies of the last 20 years, that window will close and we will bequeath to them a pessimistic future of economic and social decay.

WINDOW OF OPPORTUNITY

The human race is pivoted between tremendous progress and tremendous decay. On the evening news every night you can sometimes see both. You see a report on DNA breaking through to solve a new illness and you see a portrait of an inner city, whether it's America or somewhere else, of human beings killing each other.

Renewing American Civilization, Class 1

We must replace the welfare state with an opportunity society based on the values of freedom and the potential created by the Third Wave information revolution. I think this is the central challenge of our lifetime.

Renewing American Civilization, Class 1

This risk-taking, experimental, dynamic future cannot materialize in an America which lacks faith in itself. A strong economic policy and the development of high-technology options require that we become strongly assertive on welfare reform, crime, and foreign policy.

WINDOW OF OPPORTUNITY

Today we see a country regaining its morale and rebuilding its sense of the importance of spiritual and moral values. The scientific marvels which allow us to see the Earth from outer space are actually increasing interest in spiritual and moral life. Our age of opportunity will involve spiritual and moral, as well as physical and scientific, opportunities.

WINDOW OF OPPORTUNITY

17. SPACE:
THE NEW FRONTIER

Many of the opportunities we glimpse through our window have little to do with developments here on Earth. One of the great revolutions in our lifetime has been man's leap beyond the planet.

WINDOW OF OPPORTUNITY

National Space and Aeronautics Policy Act of 1981. . . . Title IV: Government of Space Territories—Sets forth provisions for the government of space territories, including constitutional protections, the right to self-government, and admission to statehood.

Partial text of H.R. 4286, an unsuccessful bill
sponsored by Gingrich in 1981

As people grow wealthier and the cost of space transportation comes down, spending a week's vacation on a space station or a honeymoon on the moon may become commonplace. People aboard space shuttles—the DC-3s of the future—will fly out to the Hiltons and Marriots of the solar system, and mankind will have permanently broken free of the planet.

The Futurist
June 1985

Our Nation's newborn space enterprise— a baby compared to our older steel and auto industries—may soon fall behind the Europeans and the Japanese. We will have lost our lead because we did not have the foresight to make a sound economic investment in our future—and because we thought Apollo was a circus stunt, rather than the first step along the road to freedom, hope, and opportunity.

Congressional Record
June 24, 1982

A mirror system in space could provide the light equivalent of many full moons so that there would be no need for nighttime lighting of the highways. Ambient light covering entire areas could reduce the current danger of criminals lurking in darkness.

WINDOW OF OPPORTUNITY

[NASA is] a people-heavy, obsolescent bureaucracy that has got to learn a whole lot of new approaches and new techniques. . . . We ought to start changing it tomorrow morning. We say to the Russians, "Change in 5 years a system which has been there for 80 years and was a dictatorship." Why have a softer standard for ourselves?

Interview with
Aviation Week & Space Technology
December 5, 1994

18. THE THIRD WAVE AND THE INFORMATION SOCIETY

The most powerful force changing our society is the information revolution. It is as powerful as the word "revolution" suggests.

WINDOW OF OPPORTUNITY

[Alvin and Heidi Toffler] used the term "Third Wave" because they were trying to describe a scale of change that ripples through a whole society. . . . and their argument is that the first wave of change was from hunting-gathering to agriculture. . . . The second wave of change is from agriculture to the industrial revolution. . . . and now it is the Tofflers' argument that we're into the third wave of change, which is from industry to the information revolution.

Renewing American Civilization, Class 1

You are not in the middle of the Third Wave. You're in the early stages. All the changes of your lifetime up to now are minor. My favorite comparison is that we are as developed in the Third Wave as the airplane was in 1908.

Renewing American Civilization, Class 1

The next phase of the information revolution is rising power, dropping costs, worldwide networks and real-time information. Literally, your ability . . . to carry on what will probably be slightly larger than your wrist watch, will certainly be no larger than your wallet, a capacity to interact electronically worldwide in real time. And that means when you want to know something, you'll simply tap it into the device you're carrying and you'll know it. You'll access the library immediately. You want to charge something, you'll access your bank account immediately. It will be a totally different way of thinking about handling data and relating to the whole world.

Renewing American Civilization, Class 4

Much of what we did in "Desert Storm" can only be understood as a Third Wave civilization in Toffler's language, an information age civilization, colliding with a second wave civilization with an Iraqi military built on the high end of the industrial world totally out of sync with the information world.

Renewing American Civilization, Class 4

The engineers and managers who understand the objective requirements of a high-technology future find themselves unable to articulate in moving, human terms their vision of a future with a higher standard of living and better jobs for everyone. Meanwhile, the poets, writers, and artists who can reach out so powerfully through films like *The China Syndrome* and *Norma Rae* have no understanding of the world of the future.

WINDOW OF OPPORTUNITY

19. THE RISE OF
A GLOBAL MARKET

We are the only universal country of the planet, the only country that has people from everywhere. And therefore, we ought to be the advocates of the widest global market.

Los Angeles Times
June 17, 1990

We need to create local jobs here through sales worldwide. So we have to be productive enough, creative enough, interesting enough that people all over the planet like it.

Renewing American Civilization, Class 1

We are much better off to have more IBMs and more General Motors and Fords and AT&T's that are able to be everywhere. And we're much better off to have thousands of new, small businesses that compete everywhere a jet airplane goes, and anywhere a fax machine can receive their latest advertisement.

Los Angeles Times
June 17, 1990

We must learn to compete in the world market because we cannot retreat from it. The greatest productivity, the highest value added, the widest choice of products, and the greatest take-home pay are all going to be found by competing in the world market. To retreat from competition is to accept decay. We must be tougher in negotiating with our trading partners, but our goal should be to increase American exports and to create American jobs, not to decrease imports and kill foreign jobs.

Congressional Record
January 30, 1992

The price of labor is set by south China, because that's the largest center of work force on the planet. So if you want to live seven times as well as somebody in Canton, you're going to have to be seven times as productive.

Renewing American Civilization, Class 1

I am not an advocate of the kind of blind, simpleminded adherence to free trade which crushed Great Britain between 1880 and 1914. Germany and the United States protected their industries behind high tariff walls and devoured British industries which were left open to exploitation by the British government's ideological commitment to free trade at all cost. A proper goal for a government—the British then and ours today—is the freest trade possible, given the behavior of your competitors.

WINDOW OF OPPORTUNITY

PART IV
WHAT CAN BE DONE

At the start of his first videotaped lecture in the Renewing American Civilization series—after a stirring rendition of "America the Beautiful"—Newt Gingrich states his central proposition: "There is an American Civilization. It is diverse and multiethnic. But it is in fact one civilization." It rests upon five bedrock principles: personal strength, entrepreneurial free enterprise, the spirit of invention and discovery, quality, and the lessons of American history.

Gingrich's belief in American exceptionalism and the unique destiny of Americans is the text and subtext of all his writings and teachings, but it has become even more central to his vision in recent years as he has developed his concept of personal strength as the quality that sets Americans apart from all other nationalities. In his essay in *Readings in Renewing American Civilization,* he writes that he first understood the importance of personal strength when he read *Inventing America,* Gary Wills' study of the Declaration of Independence. Paraphrasing Wills, he writes that Americans today cannot fully appreciate George Washington because his importance stems not from "a brilliant I.Q." or "a charismatic speaking style" but from his "personal integrity, his personal character, and his personal commitment." In Gingrich's mind, Washington is the archetype of the ideal American character.

Gingrich, a self-made man like Horatio Alger, whom he discusses in one of his classes, has scant respect for those who would rather whine than work. This attitude permeates the ensuing chapters, which emphasize American entrepreneurial values and a pro-active plan for the future. Gingrich advocates a decentralized health care system that gives each community—and, even better, each individual—primary responsibility for his or her own health. He will require work from all able-bodied welfare recipients, including mothers with young children, and a more stringent anticrime program to reclaim the inner city.

In effect, Gingrich sees the quality of personal strength as part of individual and community character alike. Thus national self-discipline in matters of fiscal restraint is the expression in macrocosm of the very American virtue of personal strength. Gingrich places high value on the multiethnicity of American culture, characterizing it as one of America's defining attributes, and at the same time cautions against giving one ethnic group any advantages over another. Quotas of any kind are anathema to him.

In speeches crammed with allusions to popular novels, movies, management primers, 18th-century philosophical treatises, Wal-Mart, McDonald's and even the 1913 Girl Scout Manual, Gingrich weaves all these threads into a simple, comprehensible message of American optimism and empowerment, itself representative of a distinctly American archetype. Writing in *The New Yorker,* journalist David Remnick compares him to "the middle-brow thinkers of the 19th century who won their fame explaining it all in a single volume."

Whether or not Gingrich will be able to translate his Newtonian metaphysics into the laws of the land, however, is another matter. After 16 years in Congress, he has initiated and passed no major piece of legislation that bears his name. Historically, powerful speakers have made a name for themselves by their legislative accomplishments. Gingrich is well aware of the challenge. His brainchild, the Contract with America, lays out 10 major legislative initiatives. But no matter how the political chips may fall, with his accession to the Speakership of the House, Speaker Newt Gingrich has achieved his childhood goal, his private rendezvous with destiny.

20. RENEWING AMERICAN CIVILIZATION

We have to recognize our commitment to renewing American civilization by reestablishing the reality that this is a multiethnic society, but it's one civilization. People come here to be Americans and they want to be Americans, and that implies a civilization with a set of habits and patterns.

**Speech at the Capitol,
Washington, D.C.
December 5, 1994**

The five principles of American civilization are: personal strength, entrepreneurial free enterprise, the spirit of invention and discovery, quality as described by Edwards Deming, and the lessons of American history.

Renewing American Civilization, Class 8

We need to go back and reestablish the collective memory of America and the collective memory of our humanness as a part of this process of learning the lessons of American history.

Renewing American Civilization, Class 6

As [political scientist Everett Carll] Ladd himself says, "The essential distinguishing American values all reflect a pervasive underlying individualism." In other words, you can almost see the last 200 years as a history of gradually steadily spreading the right to be an individual to more and more people.

Renewing American Civilization, Class 6

The Puritans had a deeply personal sense of commitment and connection to God. They believed that life mattered, that it was real and vital, and it was real and vital because it was a life lived for God. And the intensity of the Puritan experience is at the heart of the American cultural tradition.

Renewing American Civilization, Class 6

All Americans have the same status. . . . The only dukes in America are in jazz and baseball. We don't have hierarchical structures, and that's very important.

Renewing American Civilization, Class 6

We're not Western Europe. We stand on the shoulders of Western Europe, but we are quite different. We're more entrepreneurial. We are more open to people of all ethnic backgrounds. We're more future oriented. We have no real class system.

Renewing American Civilization, Class 1

We're not going to change America in Washington, D.C. We're going to change America one individual at a time, one family at a time, one neighborhood at a time, one church or synagogue at a time, one voluntary organization at a time, one private business at a time, and then one local government, one school board, one city council, one state legislature. And yeah, the Congress and the President are going to have a role to play in all this. . . .

**Speech at the Capitol,
Washington, D.C.
December 5, 1994**

21. AMERICAN VALUES

We don't tell the poor the truth, which is, to be middle class is to work hard. To be middle class is to do a lot of things you don't want to do. And yet the values, the rewards, the ability to live a decent life, to plan your career, to send your kids to school, to go on a nice vacation, to have a decent home, those rewards are paid for by hard work, and there is no shortcut.

Renewing American Civilization, Class 2

The person who refuses to work, who refuses to do anything, who refuses to try, will rapidly be seen as the undeserving poor; somebody who doesn't have a legitimate claim on us. . . . It goes back to . . . John Smith at Jamestown saying, "If you don't work, you don't eat."

Renewing American Civilization, Class 6

Show me a wagon train that had food stamps. Show me a wagon train that had able-bodied adults who were not working. Show me a wagon train that dealt with its criminals while allowing them to wander around committing new crimes. Show me a wagon train that taxed the productive in order to subsidize people who did not want to do a day's work.

Referring to New York Governor Mario Cuomo's
1984 Democratic Convention speech.
Congressional Record
July 23, 1984

When the welfare state finds reasons to excuse people from personal strength, it begins the process of destroying them.

Renewing American Civilization, Class 2

Perseverance is the hard work you do after you get tired of doing the hard work you already did.

Perseverance is what you do when the seventh girl turned you down for dancing and you go to the eighth girl, or boy in the modern era.

Perseverance is what happens when, in my case, I ran for Congress twice and lost. I ran a third time to win. . . .

Perseverance is what it takes to get a Ph.D. or it's what it takes to finally have saved up enough money to buy that house or to buy your first car.

Renewing American Civilization, Class 2

We have six thousand years of written historical experience in the Judeo-Christian tradition. We know that rules work. We know that learning, study, working, saving and commitment are vital. That is why Republicans would replace welfare with work, that is why Republicans would cut taxes to favor families and to encourage work, saving and job creation. As President Reagan said, we are more concerned with your destination than your origin. But the Democrats want to force individuals into groups, establish quotas and limit our future based on your genetic past.

Speech to the Republican National Convention
August 19, 1992

[The Declaration of Independence] says "We are endowed by our Creator with certain unalienable rights, among which are life, liberty and the pursuit of happiness." It talks about the right of the pursuit of happiness. There's no reference to happiness stamps—to a happiness entitlement, to happiness therapy, to happiness victimization.

Remarks to a group of state legislators
December 1994

Americans have historically preferred to focus on equality of opportunity, not equality of result. Americans have no interest in saying, "Every quarterback should be treated as if they're Joe Montana." Americans have every interest in saying, "Everybody should be allowed to try out for the team." . . . Now, in that context, Americans declare themselves prepared to countenance very substantial economic inequalities, while insisting on the importance of the ideal of equal opportunities.

Renewing American Civilization, Class 6

22. FROM PASSIVITY TO INDEPENDENCE: REPLACING THE WELFARE STATE

I am not an old-time conservative who says, "Oh, look at how they're wasting your money." I am a revolutionary centrist who's saying to you, "Look how they're destroying the lives of the people that they're sending the checks to."

Renewing American Civilization, Class 9

As Franklin Delano Roosevelt warned in the late 1930s, giving permanent aid to anyone destroys them. The fact is, we've established a principle which has created a culture of poverty that is devastating, and we have to reassert that to be a healthy, full American participant is to work.

Meet the Press
December 4, 1994

Do we help the genuinely poor, or do we risk bringing down the entire structure by redistributing income to anyone who can get into the game? . . . We are absolutely committed to helping the poor. We are absolutely committed to saving social security, but the people who built the Great Society and the people who voted for a massive redistribution of income, the people who gave us 14% inflation and a trillion-dollar debt, they simply do not want to help the poor. They want to take money out of your pocket and redistribute it to whatever welfare system they invent.

Congressional Record
April 1, 1982

Democrats traditionally have taken all the credit for their giveaways. Now that these programs have turned into Frankenstein's monsters of red tape and red ink, we should insist that they continue to take the credit for them.

Speech, "The Survival of the Two-Party System"
(Ingram Library, West Georgia College)
1976

The welfare state kills more poor people in a year than private business.

Reuters
November 15, 1994

Those of us who want to save the inner city see every person in the inner city as a citizen, fully empowered, fully strengthened. The welfare state sees them as a client, weak, helpless, a victim, somebody who can only survive if the bureaucracy takes care of them and nurtures them.

Renewing American Civilization, Class 9

If I went into a public housing project and saw people who were being subsidized, who didn't work . . . my first question to them would be: how far away is the library? I mean, explain to me why I should feel sympathy for you if you have 24 hours a day, 7 days a week, nothing to do, and you cannot find the nearest public library?

Renewing American Civilization, Class 9

I personally favor mandatory requirement of work for everybody, including women with young children.

Renewing American Civilization, Class 2

If the Congress were to focus on making D.C. a decent, humane place and let the 50 governors focus on the rest of the country, I suspect that we'd be a lot better society.

Meet the Press
December 4, 1994

More young people get more entry-level training in McDonald's than anywhere else. The tragedy of the welfare state is that its answer to McDonald's is to raise taxes and transfer the money to a Job Corps bureaucracy—even though recent studies have shown you will have a lower lifetime earning level if you go to the Job Corps than if you avoid it.

Readings in Renewing American Civilization

One of the great intellectual failures of the welfare state is its penchant for sacrifice, so long as the only people being asked to sacrifice are working, taxpaying Americans.

Readings in Renewing American Civilization

23. YOUTH IN SOCIETY

The little four-year-old who was thrown off the balcony in Chicago would have been a heck of a lot better off at Boys Town, the 11-year-old who was killed after he killed a 14-year-old might have had a chance to live in a supervised boarding school, the children you see in D.C. killed every weekend might be better off in a group home or a foster home.

I don't understand liberals who live in enclaves and safety who say, "Oh, this would be a terrible thing. Look at the Norman Rockwell family that would break up." The fact is, we are allowing a brutalization and a degradation of children in this country, a destructiveness. We say to a 13-year-old drug addict who is pregnant, you know, put your baby in a dumpster, that's okay, but we're not going to give you a boarding school, we're not going to give you a place for that child to grow up. . . .

Now, wouldn't it have been better for that girl, instead of dumping her baby in a dumpster, to have had a place she could go. . . ?

Defending his proposal that children of mothers who could not afford to support them be put in orphanages.
Meet the Press
December 4, 1994

All healthy societies understand that one of their primary goals is to train, educate and acculturate young males. The young males are the most dangerous physically, and they're the most dangerous in terms of being totally irresponsible. Because they are driven biologically to be nomadic, and to leave as many pregnant women behind as they can. And that's a biological reality.

**Speech to Young Republicans,
Washington, D.C.
March 19, 1992**

My father . . . was a foster child who was adopted as a teenager. I am adopted. We have relatives who are adopted. We are not talking out of some vague, impersonal, Dickens Bleak House, middle-class, intellectual model. We have lived the alternative.

**Speech on opening day
of the 104th Congress
January 4, 1995**

Crime is not a hard problem. We simply lock up violent criminals until they're too old to be violent. That means fewer welfare workers and more police officers and prosecutors and prisons.

"The Life of the Party,"
Policy Review
Winter 1990

I tell every young person: read lots of biographies. It's cheaper to find out in three pages how somebody else messed up than it is to mess up yourself. And it's easier to find out in 10 pages how somebody was a success than it is to try to go out and invent it yourself.

Renewing American Civilization, Class 1

The federal government is more concerned with where my children go to school than what they actually learn.

Speech announcing candidacy for Congress
(Ingram Library, West Georgia College)
March 22, 1976

How can we have a serious talk about whether or not to use American troops if nobody knows the history of the German army in Yugoslavia, which was a disaster, by the way? How can you talk seriously about the essence of America if you don't know who George Washington was, you've never heard of the Constitution, or you don't understand anything at all about Jefferson or about Hamilton or about Lincoln?

Renewing American Civilization, Class 6

. . . the real success is the morning we wake up on a Monday and no child has been killed anywhere in America that weekend, and every child is going to a school their parents think is worth attending.

Speech at the Capitol,
Washington, D.C.
December 5, 1994

24. AMERICAN DIVERSITY

Looking at a choice between progress and decay, I want to assert that only America can lead. . . . Only America is big enough, multi-ethnic enough, and committed to human freedom enough to lead.

Renewing American Civilization, Class 1

A decade of affirmative action has produced office after office in which people have their jobs because of quotas rather than competence.

WINDOW OF OPPORTUNITY

This is a nation of 260 million people, and in order to govern it, you've got to have a party big enough to attract about 160 million of 'em—160 million Americans is a pretty strange family picnic.

The Washington Blade
November 25, 1994

Conservative Republicans are . . . explicitly for integration and civil rights for everyone—but civil rights based on individual characteristics, not genetic code.

Policy Review
Winter 1991

We believe in affirmative opportunities for those from a culture of poverty or in genuine economic need. However, helping a millionaire's son or daughter because they fit the right quota, while denying the child of a low-income worker because they are in the wrong quota, is simply wrong. We also believe that any efforts to set up group politics based on quotas and set-asides is inherently destructive of that ideal.

Congressional Record
January 30, 1992

I think that on most things most days, the vast majority of practicing homosexuals are good citizens. So why would you say that of all the different groups you can pick on, this is the one group that you are going to single out? . . .

[The Republican Party's position] should be toleration. It should not be promotion and it should not be condemnation. I don't want to see police in the men's room, which we had when I was a child, and I don't want to see trying to educate kindergarteners in understanding gay couples.

The Washington Blade
November 25, 1994

It is madness to pretend that families are anything other than heterosexual couples. I think it goes to the core of how civilization functions.

The Washington Blade
November 25, 1994

25. THE ENTREPRENEURIAL SPIRIT

A society that focuses on creating wealth will find itself getting very, very rich and dramatically increasing the scale of achievement, whereas the society that focuses on redistributing wealth will rapidly discourage people from creating it.

Renewing American Civilization, Class 3

Only when the welfare state starts to break down the work ethic and the savings ethic, when it erects barriers to setting up a business and when it starts to break down the family, does entrepreneurism fail and we see ethnic groups trapped in poverty.

Readings in Renewing American Civilization

Bureaucracy, credentialing, taxation, litigation, and regulation. These are the five great enemies that killed the entrepreneurial spirit.

Renewing American Civilization, Class 3

If Thomas Edison had invented the electric light in the age of the welfare state, the Democrats would immediately introduce a bill to protect the candlemaking industry. The Democrat ticket would propose a tax on electricity—in fact, Al Gore does propose a tax on electricity. Ralph Nader would warn that electricity can kill; and at least one news report would begin, "The candlemaking industry was threatened today."

**Speech, the Republican National
Convention in Houston
August 1992**

The welfare state keeps trying to figure out a way to get 100 people to be as productive as one genius instead of figuring out how to inspire geniuses to be productive.

Renewing American Civilization, Class 4

It is dangerous to develop energy programs that focus on already gigantic companies. Asking Exxon to help develop solar power would have been like asking the Pennsylvania Railroad to help develop the automobile or asking General Motors to develop the computer. If we truly believe in small business and in free enterprise, then our government programs must reflect that faith and must encourage new business.

Speech, "The Survival of the Two-Party System"
(Ingram Library, West Georgia College)
1976

26. FIXING THE ECONOMY

If you watch carefully, you will notice that every liberal Democratic budget alternative in one way or another takes more money out of your wallet because they do not think you are bright enough to spend your own money, but if they bring it to Washington, then they can hire your brother-in-law, who magically on the trip to Washington to become a bureaucrat becomes smart enough to spend your money, although if he would return back home, he would once again be too dumb and have to give his money up to the liberal welfare state. So the first issue is, who should spend your money? We think you should. The liberal Democrats think they should.

Congressional Record
April 1, 1982

I was very surprised last night back home in a town hall meeting in Morrow, Georgia, which was on crime, to have fully a third of the people who came want to talk about crimes relating to the Internal Revenue Service and crimes relating to the Tax Code, and there was as great a plea last night welling up from this audience that had come out to talk about crime, there was as great a plea for a simplified Tax Code as there was for efforts to stop drug dealers from making our children addicts and to stop violent criminals from getting out again.

Congressional Record
May 15, 1984

In no way, under any circumstances, do I talk about abolishing Social Security. . . . I have said it is better for us to pay a tax through a sales tax than through a tax on workers, so that everybody would pay in. [This is] a change in the way you pay for it. It's not a new tax. It's a replacement of the current anti-labor, anti-work tax.

Douglas County (Ga.) Sentinel
May 10, 1988

Now, let me point out, the one Government program people actually seem to like is Social Security. . . .This is the one program also, by the way, which has a very tiny bureaucracy. We send out more Social Security checks with fewer civil servants than almost any other program in the Government. So which program do our friends in the Democratic administration want to hit? Social Security.

Congressional Record
February 2, 1993

In order to create jobs for poor Americans, we believe in the strongest possible tax incentives, including zero capital gains, a massive investment tax credit for each new job, and special tax credits for hiring the hardcore unemployed and developing special job-related apprenticeship and training programs for lower-income workers. We also recognize that inner city and rural America each have unique problems that must be resolved before prosperity can occur.

Congressional Record
January 30, 1992

We notice also that the new term in Washington is investment. Investment has replaced pork barrel. It is a good Washington word, and people who love big Government and love the welfare state believe if they run around chanting investment long enough, people will not notice that investment is just a new word for spending.

Congressional Record
February 2, 1993

We're going to get to tax cuts in the first hundred days [of the 104th Congress]. We're going to keep the contract. . . . We're going to read it as the opening speech every day. This is the campaign—this is the Contract with America—and it says we're going to bring to the floor of the House a comprehensive tax cut bill in the first hundred days, and we will.

Meet the Press
December 4, 1994

It is fascinating to me, as a conservative and someone who has been active for 24 years now since I was a high school student saying that deficits are bad, to suddenly in the last 2 years find liberal Democrats discovering deficits. It is a little bit like a large whiskey company discovering alcoholism. Suddenly liberal Democrats who believe in big Government, who love big Government, who pass every big Government program, who vote for every big Government bill, who believe deeply in spending, suddenly get up and say, "My goodness, there is a deficit." And fascinatingly enough, the deficit is always Ronald Reagan's.

Congressional Record
July 23, 1984

27. HEALTH CARE

It is astonishing to me—in this era of wide-spread and well-deserved disillusionment with big government—that so many well-informed, concerned citizens would want to nationalize and bureaucratize American medicine, some as explicitly as the highly structured National Health Service in the United Kingdom. We only need look at the postal and public school systems to learn that nationalization means neither efficiency nor economy and at the telephone system to learn that private monopolies also have their flaws.

Unidentified newspaper article
(Ingram Library, West Georgia College)
1974

There has been a 50-year-long war between the Left, which loves socialized medicine, loves coercive centralized bureaucratic power . . . and the rest of us. And they're very smart. They always conceal their greed for power in the language of love.

Mother Jones
October 1989

[The Clinton health care plan is designed] not for good health care . . . but to seize control of the health system and centralize power in Washington.

The Washington Post
December 15, 1993

A health tax on the alcohol and tobacco industries would begin to recoup the costs they impose on society at large and would have two beneficial side effects: We would marginally discourage alcohol and tobacco abuse, and we would encourage people to watch what they drink and smoke.

Policy Review
Summer 1984

First we designed a Medicare system with so much red tape that people didn't want to work with it. Then we threatened to jail people for failing to participate in a system we had fouled up. It was arrogance of big government at its worst.

Assessing a Democratic proposal that
called for the jailing of doctors who fail to obey
regulations on accepting Medicare patients.
Policy Review
Summer 1984

[Medicare is a] Harvard[-style] centralized bureaucracy-driven model of health care, which is inherently, catastrophically bad. . . . There are two realities to the current system: one is the government is trying to cheat you. And the second is the government is lying to you about what it's doing.

Mother Jones
October 1989

If a community offers to replace Medicare for its county with a different system, we should allow it. A conservative opportunity society would explicitly encourage local options, local inventions, and local experiments.

Policy Review
Summer 1984

We need a health care system where it is relatively easy for local doctors, local hospitals, and local communities to run experiments and see what will work. With a diversity of experiments in health care, we can have three or four hundred different models across the country.

Policy Review
Summer 1984

We are trying to invent marginally better iron lungs. What we need are breakthroughs that will reshape the system of health care.

Policy Review
Summer 1984

Within a decade, a combination of good health habits and home health care could reduce the total number of hospital days by 20 percent. That would save substantially more money than the bureaucratic controls we are moving toward. . . .

We may want to reward people who do not need health care.

For instance, we could simply offer a $500 year-end bonus to people who have not used Medicare during the year.

Policy Review
Summer 1984

The shortest distance between two points is a straight line, unless you're crossing a mine field. Health care reform is just such a mine field. If President Clinton brushes aside the offers of help from Republicans and decides to lead a partisan rush to comprehensive reform, it will blow up in his face, and in the ashes of that explosion will be buried the chances of genuine health care reform for another generation.

Op-ed article,
The Washington Post
March 9, 1993

28. FOREIGN POLICY AND NATIONAL DEFENSE

The American military costs too much and does too little.

The collection of overweight, out-of-touch generals and admirals, working with equally overweight, out-of-touch Congressmen, has produced an expensive and frighteningly dangerous state of weakness in our military.

The American Army could not last a weekend in Western Europe against the Russians. The Sixth Fleet could not last a full day against the Soviet fleet.

Campaign position paper
(Ingram Library, West Georgia College)
1974

The United States is in greater danger from foreign powers than at any time since the British burned the capital in 1814. American foreign policy is increasingly confused and ineffective.

The Georgian (Carrollton, Ga.)
March 18, 1976

If, in fact, we are to follow the Chamberlain liberal Democratic line of withdrawal from the planet, we would truly have tyranny everywhere and we in America could experience the joys of Soviet-style brutality and the murdering of women and children.

Congressional Record
October 27, 1983

I'm one of the leading speakers on Nicaragua. I am not a gadfly.

Responding to a claim in the *Atlanta Journal*
that he had little experience in foreign affairs.
The Atlantic Monthly
May 1985

We must expect the Soviet system to survive in its present brutish form for a very long time. There will be Soviet labor camps and Soviet torture chambers well into our great grand-children's lives: great centers of political and economic power have enormous staying power; Czarist Russia lasted through three and a half years of the most agonizing kind of war; the Nazi state did not collapse even when battlefield defeats reduced its control to only a tiny sliver of Germany.

WINDOW OF OPPORTUNITY

They're not going to go to one man, one vote in the next 15 years, and they shouldn't. All over Africa, the tradition is one man, one vote, one time. I think we ought to be more honest and say that moving from where we are to where we'd like to be may take a century.

Commenting on the white-minority
South African government.
The Atlanta Constitution
August 8, 1985

I would argue that we're caught in the tragic irony that the curve, if you will, of threat from Iraq, Iran and Syria is rising at a rate about as fast as—or faster than—the curve of Soviet threat is declining.

Los Angeles Times
June 17, 1990

The McGovern-Mondale Democrats have been wrong on every major foreign policy crisis for a decade and we have the trophies to prove it: Ho Chi Minh City instead of Saigon; death in Cambodia instead of a pro-Western government; yellow rain chemical warfare in Laos by the Soviets; Soviet troops in Afghanistan; Cuban troops in Africa, American hostages in Iran, a Communist dictatorship in Nicaragua. These were the bitter fruits of the McGovern-Mondale Democratic policies of the last decade.

Now the same men would add a Communist El Salvador, a Syrian and Soviet-controlled Lebanon, and embattled Israel, and a neutralized Persian Gulf.

Congressional Record
February 2, 1984

We should radically overhaul our entire attitude towards the United Nations. It is a failed institution in its current form. It has grotesque pretensions to be a world government. It is not a world government.

Meet the Press
December 4, 1994

I think the United States should ask General [Colin] Powell . . . to visit the Bosnian Serb leadership and to say to them, "If you launch a general offensive, we would reserve the right to use air power against every position you have. Against every command-and-control center, against every position everywhere." . . . I would do it all with air power, but I would do it like Desert Storm and I would do it like 1972 [when the U.S. bombed North Vietnam]. I would not do it when Nixon used B-52s against North Vietnam. I would not engage in this nonsensical, "you shoot one missile at us, we'll drop one bomb." This is the dumbest—this is as though Lyndon Johnson and Vietnam never occurred.

Meet the Press
December 4, 1994

If the Soviet empire still existed, I'd be terrified. The fact is we can afford a fairly ignorant presidency now.

The Atlantic Monthly
June 1993

29. TONGUE OF NEWT

People who are truly successful have some internal technique of maximizing the good luck and minimizing the bad luck. . . . I was dramatically shaped by my grandmother and my aunts because they convinced me there was always a cookie available. Deep down inside me I'm four years old, and I wake up and I think out there, there's a cookie. Every morning I'm going, you know, either it can be baked or it's already been bought, but it's in a jar . . . somewhere. . . . And so that means when you open up the cupboard and the cookie isn't there, I don't say, Gee, there's no cookie. I say, I wonder where it is.

Renewing American Civilization, Class 3

Vision must lead to words. Our vision cannot exist if we cannot say it. Strategy must lead to policies, to strategies, and they must lead to structures for implementation. Operations must be definable tasks for which we can hold people accountable. The tactics on a daily basis must be a doctrine that fits our vision of strategy.

Congressional Record
March 21, 1986

There are consistencies of pattern but not consistencies of process. You can't predict from day to day what I'll do, but you can predict from day to day what, in a general way, I'll be doing.

Comment at a meeting of his congressional
staff in April 1983. Quoted in *Roll Call*
December 12, 1994

I don't do by planning, I plan by doing.

Comment at a meeting of his congressional
staff in April 1983. Quoted in *Roll Call*
December 12, 1994

I am sort of the leading insider outsider. It is a very interesting question whether I am simply a noisier insider or still an outsider. You watch over the next few years and decide yourself.

Interview, June 16, 1990.
Quoted in *The New York Times*
July 19, 1990

A year which ends in three zeroes is a rare thing indeed. As the year 2000 approaches, more and more people will notice that they are about to celebrate something which no ancestor for nearly 30 generations saw, and which none of their successors for another 30 generations will see.

WINDOW OF OPPORTUNITY

You can now get a certificate to teach German by sitting through enough classes, but if you speak German, you can't teach German if you don't have a certificate. So you can have a German teacher who can't speak German, but though they have the certificate so they can teach, even though they can't teach. . . . If you can speak it, you can't teach it, even if you could teach it. Are you with me so far?

Renewing American Civilization, Class 4

A lot of what has happened in the modern world is that we have intellectually beaten the passion out of the system and we have become so cynical that it doesn't work. . . . You almost have to go into novels and movies and the rhythm of fiction to understand the mystery, the magic, the romance by which a free society functions, because without that mystery, again, it's like the difference between sex and love. The acts can look very similar but they're in fact remarkably different.

Renewing American Civilization, Class 10

We have to invent an entire new model, and we replace in a sense the rectangle of the liberal welfare state with the oblong of what we are currently calling the conservative opportunity society in which there will be an anticonservative opportunity society, Democratic minority, and a Republican proconservative opportunity society majority.

**Congressional Record
November 3, 1983**

Conservative books sell. I can't help it if liberal books don't sell.

Commenting on the reported $4.5 million advance he would receive for writing two books. After intense criticism, he announced that he would take just a $1 advance and royalties from actual book sales.
As reported in the *Daily News* (New York City)
December 23, 1994

30. THE NEW AGENDA

I will cooperate with President Clinton, but not compromise.

Comment made after the '94 election, when it was clear that Gingrich would be the next Speaker of the House.
Reuters
November 15, 1994

We will vote on term limits. I favor 12-year limits in the House and Senate, and I will vote for it and try to pass it.

Meet the Press
December 4, 1994

I think Social Security ought to be off limits, at least for the first four to six years.

Speech on opening day of the 104th Congress
January 4, 1995

If we're moving into the information age, don't we have to figure out how to carry the poor with us? Don't they have every right to have as much access as anybody else? I'm just tossing this out . . . but maybe we need a tax credit for the poorest Americans to buy a laptop.

Speech to the House Ways
and Means Committee.
January 5, 1995

Beyond the contract, I think there are two giant challenges. . . . One is to achieve a balanced budget by 2002. . . . Second, I think we have to find a way to truly replace the current welfare state with an opportunity society.

Speech on opening day of the 104th Congress
January 4, 1995

And I would say to my friends on the left who believe that there's never been a government program that wasn't worth keeping, you can't look at some of the the results we now have and not want to reach out to the humans and forget the bureaucracies.

Speech on opening day of the 104th Congress
January 4, 1995

EPILOGUE: A NOVEL APPROACH

Even though it had been only minutes since their last lovemaking, [he] was as ever overwhelmed by the sight of her, the shameless pleasure she took in her own body and its effect on him. Still, he mustn't let her see just how much she moved him. A relationship had to have some balance. He stretched in turn, reached over for his cigarettes and gold-plated Ronson on the Art Deco night stand with its Tiffany lamp. Since he wasn't sure what to say, he made a production out of lighting up and enjoying that first, luxurious after-bout inhalation.

His continued silence earned him a small punishment.

"Darling . . . isn't it time for you to leave?"

Playfully, to drive home the potential loss, she bit his shoulder, then kissed it better.

"Aw, hell, I don't want to . . . I wish I could just divorce Mrs. Little Goodie Two-Shoes!"

"*I* like this arrangement," she laughed softly. "Mistress to the chief of staff of the president of the United States. Nice title, don't you think? *Such* a book I could write." . . . Suddenly the pouting sex kitten gave way to Diana the Huntress. She rolled onto him and somehow was sitting athwart his chest, her knees pinning his shoulders. "Tell me, or I will make you do terri-ble things," she hissed.

**Excerpt from draft novel, entitled *1945*,
co-authored by Gingrich, as reported in
The New York Times Magazine
December 4, 1994**

APPENDIXES

APPENDIX I
CONTRACT WITH AMERICA

With considerable fanfare, the Contract with America was signed by 367 Republican candidates for the House of Representatives on the West Front of the U.S. Capitol on September 27, 1994. It became a rallying cry for Republicans in the fall elections, setting forth their vision for America. Now that they have seized control of both houses of Congress for the first time in 40 years, the Contract is the GOP's agenda for action. As promised, the Republican-dominated House passed a series of reforms spelled out in the Contract on its first day in session. Within the first 100 days of the 104th Congress, according to the Contract, votes will be taken in the House on the 10 major bills outlined in the Contract that follows. On that warm September day, all the signers of the Contract made a pledge: "If we break this contract, throw us out."

THE CONTRACT

As Republican Members of the House of Representatives and as citizens seeking to join that body we propose not just to change its policies, but even more important, to restore the bonds of trust between the people and their elected representatives. That is why, in this era of official evasion and posturing, we offer instead a detailed agenda for national renewal, a written commitment with no fine print. This year's election offers the chance, after four decades of one-party control, to bring to the House a new majority that will transform the way Congress works. That historic change would be the end of government that is too big, too intrusive, and too easy with the public's money. It can be the beginning of a Congress that respects the values and shares the faith of the American family.

Like Lincoln, our first Republican president, we intend to act "with firmness in the right, as God gives us to see the right." To restore accountability to Congress. To end its cycle of scandal and disgrace. To make us all proud again of the way free people govern themselves.

On the first day of the 104th Congress, the new Republican majority will immediately pass the following major reforms, aimed at restoring the faith and trust of the American people in their government:

First, require all laws that apply to the rest of the country also apply equally to the Congress;

Second, select a major, independent auditing firm to conduct a comprehensive audit of Congress for waste, fraud, or abuse;

Third, cut the number of House committees, and cut committee staff by one-third;

Fourth, limit the terms of all committee chairs;

Fifth, ban the casting of proxy votes in committee;

Sixth, require committee meetings to be open to the public;

163

Seventh, require a three-fifths majority vote to pass a tax increase;

Eighth, guarantee an honest accounting of our federal budget by implementing zero baseline budgeting.

Thereafter, within the first one hundred days of the 104th Congress, we shall bring to the House Floor the following bills, each to be given full and open debate, each to be given a clear and fair vote, and each to be immediately available this day for public inspection and scrutiny.

1. The Fiscal Responsibility Act

A balanced budget/tax limitation amendment and a legislative line-item veto to restore fiscal responsibility to an out-of-control Congress, requiring them to live under the same budget constraints as families and businesses.

2. The Taking Back Our Streets Act

An anti-crime package including stronger truth-in-sentencing, "good faith" exclusionary rule exemptions, effective death penalty provisions, and cuts in social spending from this summer's crime bill to fund prison construction and additional law enforcement to keep people secure in their neighborhoods and kids safe in their schools.

3. The Personal Responsibility Act

Discourage illegitimacy and teen pregnancy by prohibiting welfare to minor mothers and denying increased AFDC [Aid for Dependent Children] for additional children while on welfare, cut spending for welfare programs, and enact a tough two-years-and-out provision with work requirements to promote individual responsibility.

4. The Family Reinforcement Act

Child support enforcement, tax incentives for adoption, strengthening rights of parents in their children's education, stronger child pornography laws, and an elderly-dependent-care tax credit to reinforce the central role of families in American society.

5. The American Dream Restoration Act

A $500-per-child tax credit, begin repeal of the marriage tax penalty, and creation of American Dream Savings Accounts to provide middle-class tax relief.

6. The National Security Restoration Act

No U.S. troops under UN command and restoration of the essential parts of our national security funding to strengthen our national defense and maintain our credibility around the world.

7. The Senior Citizens Fairness Act

Raise the Social Security earnings limit, which currently forces seniors out of the work force, repeal the 1993 tax hikes on Social Security benefits, and provide tax incentives for private long-term-care insurance to let older Americans keep more of what they have earned over the years.

8. The Job Creation and Wage Enhancement Act

Small business incentives, capital gains cut and indexation, neutral cost recovery, risk assessment/cost-benefit analysis, strengthening of the Regulatory Flexibility Act and unfunded mandate reform to create jobs and raise worker wages.

9. The Common Sense Legal Reform Act

"Loser pays" laws, reasonable limits on punitive damages, and reform of product liability laws to stem the endless tide of litigation.

10. The Citizen Legislature Act

A first-ever vote on term limits to replace career politicians with citizen legislators.

Further, we will instruct the House Budget Committee to report to the floor and we will work to enact additional budget savings, beyond the budget cuts specifically included in the legislation described above, to ensure that the federal budget deficit will be less than it would have been without the enactment of these bills.

Respecting the judgment of our fellow citizens as we seek their mandate for reform, we hereby pledge our names to this Contract with America.

APPENDIX II
FIGHTING WORDS: THE GOPAC
ARSENAL

Among his many political activities, Newt Gingrich is the general chairman and guiding spirit of GOPAC, a political action committee. With an annual budget of about $2 million raised from contributors, GOPAC helps recruit and train political candidates, many of them at the state and local level, and spreads Gingrich's message on governing. As part of that effort, GOPAC distributes audio and video tapes and other materials that it believes Republican candidates will find useful. "Language, a Key Mechanism of Control," reprinted below, was distributed by GOPAC in the fall of 1990 along with an audio-cassette of a recent Gingrich lecture. In a cover letter, Gingrich noted that the 131 words on the list are "tested language from a recent series of focus groups where we actually tested ideas and language." This list was attacked by Democrats and was the subject of blistering newspaper editorials. *The New York Times* said the list represented "the politics of slash and burn" and represented "the worst of American political discourse." Former President Gerald Ford resigned as honorary chairman of GOPAC shortly after the list was distributed, although a spokesperson said the timing was "coincidental."

Language: A Key Mechanism of Control

As you know, one of the key points in the GOPAC tapes is that "language matters." In the video "We Are a Majority," Language is listed as a key mechanism of control used by a majority party, along with Agenda, Rules, Attitude and Learning. As the tapes have been used in training sessions across the country and mailed to candidates we have heard a plaintive plea: *"I wish I could speak like Newt."*

That takes years of practice. But, we believe that you could have a significant impact on your campaign and the way you communicate if we help a little. That is why we have created this list of words and phrases.

This list is prepared so that you might have a directory of words to use in writing literature and mail, in preparing speeches, and in producing electronic media. The words *and* phrases are powerful. Read them. Memorize as many as possible. And remember that, like any tool, these words will not help if they are not used.

While this list could be the size of the latest "College Edition" dictionary, we have attempted to keep it small enough to be readily useful yet large enough to be broadly functional. The list is divided into two sections: Optimistic Positive Governing words and phrases to help describe your vision for the future of your community (your message) and Contrasting words to help you clearly define the policies and record of your opponent and the Democratic party.

Please let us know if you have any other suggestions or additions. We would also like to know how you use the list. Call us at GOPAC or write with your suggestions and comments. We may include them in the next tape mailing so that others can benefit from your knowledge and experience.

Optimistic Positive
Governing Words

Use the list below to help define your campaign and your vision of public service. These words can help give extra power to your message. In addition, these words help develop the positive side of the contrast you should create with your opponent, giving your community something to vote *for*!

share	debate	care (ing)
change	compete	tough
opportunity	active (ly)	listen
legacy	we / us / our	learn
challenge	candid (ly)	help
control	humane	lead
truth	pristine	vision
moral	provide	success
courage	liberty	empower
reform	commitment	(ment)
prosperity	principle (d)	citizen
crusade	unique	activist
movement	duty	mobilize
children	precious	conflict
family	premise	light

dream	environ-	confident
freedom	ment	incentive
peace	reform	hard work
rights	workfare	initiative
pioneer	eliminate	common
proud / pride	good-time	sense
building	in prison	passionate
preserve	strength	
pro- (issue)	choice / choose	
flag,	fair	
children,	protect	

Contrasting Words

Often we search hard for words to define our opponents. Sometimes we are hesitant to use contrast. Remember that creating a difference helps you. These are powerful words that can create a clear and easily understood contrast. Apply these to the opponent, their record, proposals and their party.

decay	deeper	destructive
failure (fail)	crisis	destroy
collapse (ing)	urgent (cy)	sick

pathetic	waste	insensitive
lie	corruption	status quo
liberal	incompetent	mandate (s)
they/them	permissive	taxes
unionized	attitude	spend (ing)
bureaucracy	destructive	shame
"compassion"	impose	disgrace
is not	self-serving	punish
enough	greed	(poor...)
betray	ideological	bizarre
consequences	insecure	cynicism
limit (s)	anti - (issue)	cheat
shallow	flag, family,	steal
traitors	child, jobs	abuse of
sensationalists	pessimistic	power
endanger	excuses	machine
coercion	intolerant	bosses
hypocrisy	stagnation	obsolete
radical	welfare	criminal rights
threaten	corrupt	red tape
devour	selfish	patronage

APPENDIX III
MASTERS OF THE
REVOLUTION

Newt Gingrich has always read widely and drawn from many aspects of American popular culture to develop his message. In recent years, a number of contemporary writers and thinkers have had a profound impact on him. They are an eclectic lot—futurists, business consultants and experts on organizational behavior, motivational psychologists—who share no particular political views. Indeed, some of Gingrich's gurus have no discernible political outlook, while others could be classified as liberals. Here's a brief look at some of the figures who have helped shape Gingrich's political and social philosophy:

The Gurus

W. Edwards Deming: Detroit auto executives first learned about Edwards Deming in the late

1970s on trips to Japan to try and figure out how Japanese automakers were outperforming them in car design and quality. Deming, who died at age 93 in late 1993, played a key role in guiding Japan's war-shattered industries to preeminence. But only in his eighties, after establishing a name for himself in Japan, did the statistician and academic who never held a full-time job in a corporation become known in America. Ford was one of the first major U.S. corporations to recognize Deming's expertise in "quality management." (One result was a new ad slogan: Quality Is Job One.) But Deming went on to advise hundreds of companies and become the most sought-after quality expert in the nation. His key insight was that quality had to be infused into every step of the manufacturing process, even at the expense of short-term profits. In his book *Out of Crisis* (1986) he enumerated 14 points to improve quality. (Point 1: "Create constancy of purpose for improvement.") In Demings' view, the worker should be a company's most valuable asset and a company's highest purpose should be to please its customers, not its shareholders.

Alvin and Heidi Toffler: They met in 1948 when they were both student radicals and two decades later Alvin penned *Future Shock,* the best-seller that made him famous. The book argued that the ever-quickening pace of social and technological change was creating "shattering stress and disorientation" for many Americans. To cope, he called for grass-roots "democratic constituent assemblies" that would set priorities for specific social goals.

The Tofflers have gone on to develop the argument further, helping to found the World Future Society and writing other books. Gingrich is most enamored with "Creating a New Civilization: The Politics of the Third Wave," a 100-page distillation of *The Third Wave.* In this small book, Gingrich says, "you'll begin to sense what 21st-century America, the 21st-century government and the 21st-century Congress needs to be." As the Tofflers see it, civilization is in the midst of a cataclysmic change as it metamorphoses from a Second Wave industrial phase to a Third Wave phase, in which the economy is based on high tech, information and the service sector. (The First Wave phase was based on agriculture.) The role of government, the Tofflers argue, is to anticipate the ramifications of this new change by reversing the economic and political bias in favor of Second Wave industry and help smooth the way toward the future. They are optimistic about the transformation. "The Third Wave," Alvin Toffler writes, "is for those who think the human story, far from ending, has only just begun."

Peter Drucker: Drucker is the author of *The Effective Executive,* one of the books on Gingrich's required reading list. In *The Economist*'s 1993 year-end "Good Guru Guide," Drucker placed second in a field of 17, trailing slightly behind economist Milton Friedman. Born in Vienna in 1909, Drucker fled the Nazis before settling in the United States, where he has taught economics and politics and turned out more than 25 books, mostly on management. Many of his insights are now accepted as conventional wisdom. He coined the term "management by objectives." He has been advocating the privatization of Government-run industries since the 1960s and believes strongly in corporate decentralization and empowering workers. In *The Ef-*

fective Executive, he observes that "knowledge workers" (i.e., those who use their brains rather than brawn) are hard to supervise because their output is difficult to measure. He offers some commonsensical management advice, such as "The effective executive focuses on contribution." But many of his writings have great historical sweep and occasional references to Jane Austen, one of his heroines. Critics tend to dismiss Drucker as a popularizer (which he is) with a fondness for glittering generalizations. The bromide-loving Gingrich is more respectful.

Morris Shechtman: Shortly after he was tapped to be the Republican leader, Gingrich asked Shechtman, a conservative management consultant, psychotherapist and author *(Working Without a Net: How to Survive and Thrive in Today's High-Risk Business World)* to come and speak to GOP legislators about how to articulate the Republicans' social agenda without appearing insensitive. And speak Shechtman did—for six hours. Shechtman makes the case that Corporate America's biggest problem is denial. "In organizations," he writes, "denial is in full bloom when a manager deals with an incompetent subordinate by saying, 'Don't worry about it; just give him some time.' People don't spontaneously recover from incompetence." He applies his book's "compassion-can-be-destructive message," as one book reviewer has aptly called it, to society-at-large as well. In his talk to legislators, Shechtman argued that the nation's welfare system does more harm than good. "What the country has been doing for three decades in the guise of helping people has literally hurt and killed people," he said. He's particularly critical of affirmative action, which, he said, "has created a world in which you can sue to get a job with someone who considers you to be a turkey. Clinically, we call that sadomasochism." Like Gingrich, he favors social programs that make people more responsible for themselves. Gingrich plans to invite Shechtman back to Washington so that every member of Congress has the chance to attend one of his seminars.

Mary E. Boone: Her message is straightforward: "I try to convey to managers and top executives that computers are more than just administrative tools," she told a recent interviewer. "They are powerful tools for leadership and for motivation." To spread the computer gospel, Boone wrote *Leadership and the Computer: Top Executives Reveal How They Personally Use Computers to Communicate, Coach, Convince and Compete.* The book includes interviews with 17 corporate leaders—including Debi Fields of Mrs. Fields Cookies and Ron Compton, chief executive of Aetna Life & Casualty—and several major computer companies helped finance Boone's research. After the book caught Gingrich's interest, he invited the 35-year-old management consultant down for breakfast. "This is more than about what computer do I buy," Gingrich said recently in recommending the Boone book to his fellow legislators. He gives the book credit for suggesting to him, among other things, the possibility of creating "a virtual Congress where we can have hearings in five cities by television while the actual committee is sitting here." Indeed, on his first day as Speaker, Gingrich took a step toward bringing Congress into the information age by making Congressional bills and reports available by computer so, as he put it, "every citizen has the same instantaneous access as the highest-paid lobbyist in Washington, D.C."

Newt Gingrich is, of course, a man of many theories, and the number of people and ideas that influence him is constantly expanding. The anthology *Readings in Renewing American Civilization,* for which Gingrich wrote the introduction, includes nine other contributors, many of whom are well-known in conservative intellectual and political circles and are often given credit for influencing Gingrich's thoughts. Everett Carll Ladd, a political scientist and director of the Roper Center for Public Opinion Research, contributed an essay on "The American Ideology"; George Keyworth, President Reagan's former science adviser, wrote on "The Spirit of Invention and Discovery"; and Arianna Huffington, wife of the defeated California senatorial candidate, opined on "Twelve Steps to Cultural Renewal." There's a contribution, too, from Stephen R. Covey, author of the best-selling *7 Habits of Highly Effective People,* on "Personal Strength in American Culture." Besides being a favorite of Gingrich, Covey was recently summoned to Camp David to have a chat with President Clinton. Time will tell which politician was the better listener.

REQUIRED READING LIST

Never at a loss for words, Newt Gingrich talked for an hour after being unanimously chosen by his fellow House Republicans to be the next Speaker on December 5, 1994. In the course of his talk, he suggested that his colleagues read the following documents and books:

The Declaration of Independence

The Federalist Papers

Democracy in America,
   Alexis de Tocqueville

Washington: The Indispensable Man,
   James T. Flexner

Creating a New Civilization:
   The Politics of
   the Third Wave,
   Alvin and Heidi Toffler

The Effective Executive,
   Peter F. Drucker

Leadership and the Computer,
   Mary E. Boone

Working Without a Net:
   How to Survive and Thrive in
   Today's High-Risk Business World,
   Morris R. Shechtman

SOURCE INFORMATION

In researching this book, we consulted a wide array of published and unpublished materials, transcripts and campaign papers. We would like to acknowledge the following sources.

UNPUBLISHED MATERIAL

Transcript of Newt Gingrich speech to the Republican National Convention. August 18, 1992. Provided by the Republican National Committee.

Transcripts and videotapes of Renewing American Civilization, taught by Gingrich at Reinhardt College, January–February 1994. Provided courtesy of The Progress & Freedom Foundation.

Compilation of Newt Gingrich quotes. Provided by the Democratic National Committee.

Meet the Press transcript, December 4, 1994. NBC News.

Interview with *U.S. News & World Report*. Republican National Convention, August 19, 1992. U.S. News & World Report.

Transcript of speech to House Republicans, December 5, 1994. Federal News Service.

Personal papers of David Worley.

Claxton Collection, Ingram Library, West Georgia College, Carrollton, Ga. The archive contains numerous speeches, position papers and campaign documents.

PUBLISHED MATERIAL

The Congressional Record

Contract with America, Republican National Committee

Georgia newspapers and magazines:

The Atlanta Journal-Constitution

Atlanta Magazine

Douglas County Sentinel

The Georgian

Rome Christian News

Rural Georgia Magazine

West Georgia News

Other newspapers, magazines, wire services, etc.:

Associated Press

The Atlantic Monthly

Aviation Week & Space Technology

The Boston Globe

The Futurist Magazine

The Heritage Foundation

Los Angeles Times

Los Angeles Times Magazine

Mother Jones

National Public Radio

NBC News
New York *Daily News*
The New Yorker
The New York Times
The Philadelphia Inquirer
Policy Review
Reuters
Roll Call
U.S. News & World Report
Vanity Fair
The Wall Street Journal
The Washington Blade
The Washington Post
The Washington Times

Books:

Changing of the Guard, by David Broder, Simon & Schuster, New York City, 1980

Creating a New Civilization: The Politics of the Third Wave, by Alvin and Heidi Toffler, The Progress & Freedom Foundation, Washington, D.C., and Atlanta, Ga., 1994

Readings in Renewing American Civilization, edited by Jeffrey A. Eisenrach and Albert Stephen Hanser, McGraw Hill Inc., 1993

Window of Opportunity, by Newt Gingrich with David Drake and Marianne Gingrich. A TOR Book, published by Tom Doherty Associates, Inc., in association with Baen Enterprises, Inc., New York City, 1984